Bruce Lee

Isometric Exercise Routines for a Bruce Lee Body

(The Truth About Bruce Lee's Life and Martial Arts Success Revealed)

Abigail Stroman

Published By **Jordan Levy**

Abigail Stroman

Bruce Lee: Isometric Exercise Routines for a Bruce Lee Body (The Truth About Bruce Lee's Life and Martial Arts Success Revealed)

ISBN   978-1-998769-04-9

Legal & Disclaimer

The information contained in this ebook is not designed to replace or take the place of any form of medicine or professional medical advice. The information in this ebook has been provided for educational & entertainment purposes only.

The information contained in this book has been compiled from sources deemed reliable, and it is accurate to the best of the Author's knowledge; however, the Author cannot guarantee its accuracy and validity and cannot be held liable for any errors or omissions. Changes are periodically made to this book. You must consult your doctor or get professional medical advice before using any of the suggested remedies, techniques, or information in this book.

Table Of Contents

Chapter 1: Kung Fu Fighting

It was the decade that saw platform shoes, bellbottoms, and white discosuits. But something else was making a splash. What was it called? Kung Fu. The martial arts world was in full swing, and there was no stopping this madness.

For a better understanding of the Kung Fu universe, buckle up and join us for a ride to 1970s.

Kung Fu was a television program. David Carradine played Kwai Chang, a Shaolin Monk who travels the American Wild West using only his spiritual trainings and kick-ass martial arts skills. I bet you and your grasshopper' friends remember watching the show when you were a kid.

Kung Fu Fighting, a disco-ditty, rose high in the charts. The song rode the wave of martial arts like a Ninja surfboarding, and quickly made its way to number one in the UK as well as the US. Anyone who heard Carl Douglas' song would be able to identify the lyrics as indelibly embedded on their brains. "Everybody was kung Fu fighting." These cats were quick as lightning." The song won a Grammy. It would go on sale over 11 million times worldwide.

Kung Fu influence was everywhere in comic-books. Marvel magazine had ShangChi -- The Master and Son of Fu Manchu. Iron Fist, my personal favourite was next. Roy Thomas and Gil Kane made Iron Fist. Thomas wrote that they had... started it because I'd seen my very first kung Fu movie. It had something called 'The Ceremony of the Iron Fist.' It seemed like a good name. We already had Master of Kung Fu. However, I thought it was a good idea.

* And then there was the cartoons. These included Hanna-Barbera's Hong Kong Phooey. Henry, the mild-mannered police station clerk and "number 1 super guy" is something that everyone will remember from the 1970s.

Was there really a tidal wave?

First international martial arts star was the man who did a hang five from its frothy top. His name was Bruce Lee. Bruce Lee.

CHAPTER 2: Get ready to be a Dragon

"I will never forget my first two weeks in New York, when I trudged the streets looking for a partner for Kung-Fu Monthly. My hair was half-down. My high-heeled Snakeskin boots, Mr Fish tie, and Tommy Nutter knockoff suits were not the American businessmen I was used to.

This is the story on how a struggling UK publisher put Bruce Lee's picture on millions upon millions of bedroom walls. 1974 was the year Felix Dennis was trying to find his first true financial success. He was unaware of the success that would come with Kung-Fu Monthly's publication, a poster-magazine on Bruce Lee.

Dennis sent Don Atyeo his friend to Hong Kong after Bruce Lee's death to interview anyone who was familiar with the star. These interviews and the hundreds of Bruce Lee photographs obtained would become the basis of the monthly magazine. Dennis would find the perfect photos, even though he was unaware of it.

Empire of the Dragon

Dennis's distributors had given the magazine for one year prior to its collapse. As it turned out, hippy journalists who were ignorant about kung fu could only publish one man each year. Kung-Fu Monthly didn't cease publication after twelve months. This surprised everyone. Instead, it was published for ten consecutive years.

How did this happen? Dennis had a few tricks up his sleeves:

* First, Bruce Lee lived quickly and died young, cementing his legacy among Hollywood stars like Marilyn Monroe, James Dean, and James Dean.

* Second, the martial arts were very popular in practically every country around the globe, even the Third World.

* Thirdly Dennis was passionately interested in this new magazine format, and bravely overcame any obstacles.

What follows?

Dennis leapt onto planes to see countries after the magazine had been published. Soon the mag would be published in

German French, Italian Swedish, Dutch, Spanish, Arabic, and Swedish.

The flood of success brought it all. Bruce Lee would build a publishing empire worth millions by publishing one magazine after the next.

Picture Perfect

You can hang posters on walls. That was the secret. It was the unusual format of a monthly magazine that allowed kids to hang it on the wall after finishing reading each month's issue.

You are likely to have owned one or more posters from this era if you grew-up in it. This concept was brilliant. It was perfect. It ensured that Bruce Lee's famous physique could be seen on bedrooms all around the world.

Bruce Lee, a martial artist from the pre-internet age of before Twitter and Facebook became viral.

Feeding Frenzy

Randy Pausch, Professor in Computer Science, said that luck is where preparation meets chance. Dennis, a maverick publisher was fortunate to be at the right spot and time to enjoy the kung-fu feeding frenzy of over a decade.

How influential was Kung-Fu Monthly!

Dennis continued to fend the kung fury flames for ten more years, until they could rival the fiery breaths of the most powerful dragon. Everyone wanted to be a kung Fu fighter like Bruce Lee.

To fulfill their desire, Bruce Lee's fans would join self-defense classes in the United States and look for Bruce Lee workouts and methods.

In Chapter 3, we'll show you how Bruce Lee's body has survived scrutiny to this day and still holds onto its legendary status.

Chapter 2: Bruce Lee Body

Bruce Lee, the martial artist, would most likely be near the top of any list of muscular men from history. Joe Weider, bodybuilding magnate, said that Lee had the "most defined body I have ever seen" because of his muscle mass.

And the awards don't end there. Lee Haney and Lou Ferrigno would be inspired by his physique. Dorian Yates was also influenced six times Mr. Olympia. Most remarkable of all is the fact that "Little Dragon", who stood 5ft 8in tall in his stocking feet, weighed in at just 140 pounds.

What is Bruce Lee's secret to bodybuilding? The secret is quality.

Bruce Lee Physique

This quality is what has allowed Bruce Lee to maintain his physique and remain iconic. Lee, who is considered to have the perfect combination of muscle definition, muscularity and amazing symmetry, would create a body with a rippled and bulging appearance that looks like it was made from granite.

The extremely low body fat percentage helped to further enhance this incredible conditioning. How much body weight did Lee have? The minimum amount of essential fat that a male should have is 3%, according to exercise physiologists. This is an important number, because even in starvation this figure does not decrease as the body fights against losing its vital organs. In essence, a bodyfat percentage of 3% (or less) is equivalent to "zero".

This figure can be compared to the 2.4% recorded by Clarence Bass (author and bodybuilder) at Lovelace Medical Centre. Based on this figure, it is reasonable to infer that Lee, who was extraordinarily lean, had a lower body fat percentage than 3%.

Bruce Lee Body Statistics

Lee proved that you don't need to be huge in order to build a strong physique.

* Chest: 44

* Biceps: 14 1/2

* Forearm: 12 1/2

* Wrist: 6 1/2

* Waist: 29 1/2

* Thigh: 22 1/2

* Calves: 13

* Weight: 140 pounds

* Height: 8 feet.

However, these figures are only part of the story. These figures don't reflect the Bruce Lee physique.

Indeed, those who had worked out with Lee occasionally -- pound by pound -- said that Lee could have been one of most powerful men on the planet.

Bruce Lee, Body Strength

1. Lee was invited to California's Long Beach Karate Championships 1964 to perform his "One Inch Punch". Bob Baker of Stockton was his opponent. Lee later said that he had told Bruce not to perform this type demonstration again. I couldn't bear to be punched by him again that time.

2. Lee's striking speed of 3 feet away was measured at 5 centiseconds. This explains why Lee would often fly to opponents twice his own size.

3. Lee repeated his 2-finger pressups at the Championships.

4. Lee had such strength that he was able to hold a 125 pound barbell at arm's length for several second.

5. Bruce Lee can perform 50 one-arm, chin ups in a show of his fitness.

6. Lee was a display of power by putting his fingers through open Coca-Cola cans!

Bruce Lee had a strong physique, was lightning fast and had virtually no body fat. How the hell did he do that? The key lies in the next chapter, which will show us the way to mastery.

Chapter 3: The Path To Mastery

George Leonard recounts the story of Jigora Kanot, who is considered the father of judo in his book Mastery. According to legend, Kano was close to death when he called his students together and requested that they be buried under his white belt.

It is a strange thing that the highest-ranking martial artist of his discipline would wear the emblem for the novice. It's quite simple. Kano says that mastery is never finished.

Your Path to Mastery

The path to mastery requires you to give the best of yourself to your most important work. The last part of this statement is worth special mention. Why? You see, mastering the right thing can make all things seem easier.

Here are the reasons why mastering what you love is so important.

In the next chapters I'll be discussing this concept. How simplicity and Tao can help you train -- if you are able to focus on one thing, it can lead to powerful results.

Bruce Lee was a martial artist who realized this early on in his career. He used laser beams to help him with his weight training, as part of his quest for mastery.

Your pathway to elite performance

K. Anders Ericsson's study into elite performance is a good example of mastery. His findings revealed how elite performers become elite by deliberate practice over a number of years. Ericsson's findings would debunk the prodigy myth and show that talent is not enough. Practice is key to success.

Practice alone is not enough.

It is essential to understand the fundamental elements of what you are doing to be a master at weight training and other activities. Only then can your first steps be taken towards mastery and elite performance.

Your speed increases, and your confidence grows. As your confidence grows and you become more competent, you will be amazed to discover that the first steps to mastery do not differ from one pursuit to another.

Why? It's because mastery allows you to open yourself up to other possibilities. Like a tumbling donut knocking over another domino, knowledge builds on knowledge. Skills build on knowledge. For that to happen you need to be hungry for knowledge and become a student in exercise science like Bruce Lee, a 20th-century boy.

Chapter 4: 20th Century Boy

Marc Bolan's 20th Century Boy song said, "Move as a cat, charge as a ram, sting just like I feel -- babe! I want to be your man!" T-Rex's chart-buster could have been written just for Bruce Lee. The UK reached number 3 with the 1973 March release. This was a hip, confident, and cocky song that quickly became a classic 70s soundtrack.

This being said, who could have foreseen Lee's shocking passing that fateful summer.

The answer is not in anyone. Why? Because this 20th century boy, confident and cocky, stood proudly at a zenith.

Lee was not just a film star or a martial arts artist. He was also a student and researcher in exercise science. His thirst for knowledge would lead to a strength training regimen where each exercise was thoroughly tested for its effectiveness.

Lee's personal library numbered well over 2500 books. It was a collection that included both current writings and the works of past bodybuilders, including Eugene Sandow. Lee was meticulous in his training, focusing on all elements of total strength, muscle endurance, flexibility, and cardiovascular endurance.

How to Train Dragons

Lee's drive to reach his full potential made it possible for him to continually improve his weight-training. He placed particular emphasis on his arms. Lee would perform single biceps curls using over 70 pounds of weight and do 50 one-arm chinups.

Lee was able to perform static contractions (isometrics), and he could also hold a 125 pound weight barbell at his elbow. Lee's arm training continued with more arm exercises, which included wrist curls and custom-built equipment to improve his grip.

Lee quickly found the perfect workout that aligned with his philosophy of achieving maximum results for the lowest energy expenditure. Lee could not only train his muscles but also strengthen his connective tissues, such as ligaments and tendon, with just a few exercises.

Lee was not like most of his peers and wasn't concerned about muscle size or vanity. Lee wanted to train for function, which is what he believed was the most important thing. Lee was driven by this goal and decided to do the following workout.

1. Clean & Press

2. Squats

3. Pullovers

4. Bench Press

5. Good Mornings

6. Barbell Curls.

This routine served Lee very well from 1965 to 1970. Lee had already abandoned the traditional marathon training methods and was now able to do the above exercises for only 2 sets and 8-12 repetitions. Lee's goal in muscle building was to be efficient and short.

Bruce Lee's training program for barbells included the squat as the most important movement. He was well-versed in the merits and practiced the exercise strictly and consistently.

These same articles emphasized the benefits of pullingovers and squats. There is no evidence Lee did superset pullovers alongside squats. However, there is every reason for us to believe that this is possible, since pullovers were thought to be a powerful rib expander as well as a good accompaniment to deep breathing exercises like squats. Lee would be a great fan of this dynamic duo like J. C. Hise or Roger Eells.

The student of science would very soon be looking for the ultimate strength training, and would find it in the safe care of a circus strongman.

Chapter 5: Russia With Love

"I began now to think a lot regarding developing great strength within my fingers...I bent thick, green, twigs with the help of my hands. These were much better than dry, unbending wood that would break quickly. I practiced this for a long time until my hands were strong enough to bend small trees and branches. I also tried lifting stones off of the ground with my thumbs, fingers, and carrying them in my grasp for a short distance.

-- Alexander Zass

How many boys have dreams of joining the circus? One lucky Lithuanian boy would have the opportunity to fulfill this dream when he was a teenager in the early 20th century.

Meet Alexander Zass. He is widely considered the pioneer of isometric exercises and is now visiting the circus alongside his grandfather. One thing will impress him more than all the other exciting sights and sounds he's about to experience: What is it exactly? The strongman. As the youngster holds him in mesmerizing awe, he makes a heartfelt promise to one day join the circus and become an independent strongman.

It would seem simple to dismiss this childish folly. Alexander kept his word. He began strength training as soon as he could. His training program was not very well-rounded and included activities such as tree climbing and carrying heavy stones. However, his efforts paid off when he realized his boyhood ambition.

Alexander began to tour Russia with his circus act when the opportunity presented itself to him. His show included feats like bending bars and breaking chains, transporting small horses, and lifting 500-pound girders with just his teeth. Despite all his bravura, the boy of the Baltic did not lose sight the important elements he considered key. What were they exactly? They were the wrists or hands.

Super-Humanly strong

According to the Lithuanian strongman you need to focus on your wrists and hands if you want to be super-humanly strong. These were seen as weak links in people and the training they received often made the difference of a strongman from a normal man. Alexander believed that this belief motivated him to practice his grip and strengthen the supporting tendons, ligaments, and muscles.

What are his methods of training? He was a fierce advocate for isometric exercises and trained with handles that were connected to large, heavy chains. Alexander explained the many benefits of this system of training by saying that it would store energy, not dissipate it, and increase stamina. Exercise against very strong resistance is the only method I know.

The events would soon take a dramatic turn for worse. Alexander's training system was put through its paces while he served in the Russian army during World War 1.

The Great Escape

If you read our story like a Hollywood script, then the next part would be a great fit for a blockbuster movie screenplay.

Alexander Zasss was arrested by the Austrians and taken into custody during the Great War. Alexander, who was held in prison and bound by chains, feared losing the strength and size he had worked for. In desperate times, he started pulling against the prison bars and the chains that bound Alexander. Alexander's surprise was complete when he realized that this type training helped him not only to keep his strength but also to become stronger.

What did you do next?

The circus strongman broke his chains using his only hands before ripping out the bars on his prison windows.

After his wartime heroics, "Mighty Samson," a popular book about the extraordinary bodybuilding benefits isometric exercise has published. Bruce Lee's library shelves had one copy. As both strongmen had a passion to do this ultimate strength exercise, I believe so.

The next chapter will discuss the unique characteristics that make this system such a powerful tool.

Chapter 6: Tao Of Training

"Practicing Tao builds daily simplification. There will never be any striving, so there will be less of it. It is possible to accomplish everything when effort is not resorted to. By not interfering with the world, one wins it. "One who interferes with the world will lose it."

-- Lao-Tzu (604 BC - 531 BC)

Welcome to Tao. This Chinese concept roughly translates as 'way' or'method' or 'principle. It signifies either the fundamental nature of all things or the order and natural order of them.

These situations allow Tao to convey the idea of simplicity, power, and almost magical effectiveness.

Bruce Lee's teaching philosophy clearly demonstrates this simple but powerful effectiveness. Lee's training philosophy is based on the core moves for bodybuilding and consists of the fundamental principles or Tao.

What does this all mean?

Lee simply does the core bodybuilding exercises such as deadlifts, deadlifts, and squats.

In a moment I will show how to apply these principles to training. The result? Dragon-taming rituals are optimized for efficiency.

I am going to show you a very special razor to help you on your journey.

Occam's Razor meets Tao

Occam's Razor (or Occam's Razor) is a minimalist law. It states that the most simple answer is often correct. With a knife as sharp as the Ninja Dragon Star, Occam's Razor states that things shouldn't be complicated and that more is better.

This amazing law is everywhere. This law is commonly used to help you cut through any problem or situation, eliminating any unnecessary elements. It can also influence the way that you see the world.

Is this law possible to simplify training? Yes. It can. It can. Perhaps even more importantly, it can.

Again, the answer to this question is a resounding YES. Here is what you should do:

Similar to how a doctor might use this principle in order to determine if a patient has a specific illness, so can we do the same with our training. This process of deductive simplifying is what lies at both the core of Tao and the dragon heart for exercise selection.

The World's Most Effective Exercise

Now that you've seen some of the amazing capabilities of Occams Razor, let us spend some time together in the company of perhaps The World's Most Effective Exercise.

Chapter 7: Beauty Of The Beast

If you have had any experience with weight lifting, you'll be able to deduce the beastly move I'm about to share. The squat is a beast of burden that Mike Mentzer, an acclaimed bodybuilder, said.

"The deadlift is an excellent exercise for overall growth as it works every muscle of the backside, from the Achilles tendon through to the occiput. Deadlifts can also be used to work the deltoids, forearms, as well as every muscle in your body.

Impressive, huh? How about Stuart McRobert?

"Doing high-intensity bentleg or stiff-legged Deadlifts once per week is a great step in making big gains and to injury-free training."

Later, we'll learn how to perform isometric deadlifts, but for now, let me share 3 ways you can use this bodybuilding sledgehammer.

Number of the Beast

1. Deadlift protocol. The average trainee can do a single set of deadlifts, which is progressively worked. How often should this be done? Stuart McRobert suggests deadlifting at least once per week, and slowly adding weight to your barbell. But for some people, even this training plan may prove too challenging. If you are one of these people, you can deadlift once every ten to fifteen days or every other weekend. This is where you can benefit from the principle Tao by doing only what is necessary.

2. Swap your squats. One option that many have found very successful is the replacement of the squat by the deadlift. This makes deadlift training the mainstay of their strength training routine. A trainee

may find it difficult to do their best work or is limited in their recovery ability, so replacing one proven mass-builder makes perfect sense.

3. The best training technique. People fear the deadlift. The solution? You can show the barbell deadlift respect. Correct deadlift technique will increase your training experience as well as delivering the results you work hard in the gym. Correct deadlift technique will ensure your lower back is protected, which is crucial in building strength. Correct form will lead to increased mass and might.

Are there any deadlift routines that utilize the principle Tao for their effectiveness? This is the secret to Mother Russia's best martial arts master.

Chapter 8: The Ussr Is Back

"The Russian soldier has the best physical and mental characteristics for war. They are strong, durable, insensitive, and can withstand all the hardships that campaigning brings. They eat large quantities of raw and uncooked food. Their physical constitution is so tough that they will swim in rivers even in the coldest weather.

-- The Military Experience at the Age of Reason

Christopher Duffy

Mother Russia welcomes you back! However, before you think her soldiers can be as tough as old boot skin, we'll confirm your suspicions and call on another warmongering Soviet. His name? Pavel Tsatsouline, instructor in martial arts fitness.

This Soviet comrade demonstrated what was possible when he used only two basic lifts in his ultra-absurd routine. He was also a strong advocate for isometrics muscle tension.

But hang on. Are you sure that all the muscles are needed to build a strong body?

Yes. Yes. Do you know that simple moves such as the deadlift or press can provide all of the muscle building and functional firepower your body could need?

Our master of martial arts would also agree. Pavel Tsatsouline explains: "Build up respectable pounds on your fundamental lifts -- and you will force the lazy muscles to do their part!"

It means you can put down the isolation exercises of pea shooter and embrace the artillery cannon power inherent in core bodybuilding moves such the deadlift.

Take a look at these deadlift advantages:

1. Establish the posterior chain.

2. Strengthen your core

3. Forge a gorilla grip.

Wait... the deadlift is so great, why aren't more people practicing it in gyms

Two reasons immediately spring up in my head:

* Many trainees do not exercise their lower body, and instead focus on the more visible muscles like the biceps. If they do train their legs they will often do scary-cat extension of the legs.

* Most gym-goers are scared of deadlifts. Why? Why?

If you ignore this exercise, you may miss many of your deadlift benefits.

This is a terrible thing!

Simple answer, arrows a Kung Fu Kick direct to your Solar Plexus. Repeat after me:

It is not worth spending more when you can get the same results with less.

Power to the People

It is easy to follow. Tao training is easy with only two core exercises.

We have already discussed that the deadlift can't address one problem: your pressing prowess. To finish your deadlift, you need to add one pressing move to the exercise.

Tsatsouline wrote in Power to the People: "I prefer the old-fashioned side presses over the bench and comparable exercises." This is the perfect way to increase your muscular development.

Try this:

1. Deadlift

2. One-arm dumbbell press

Or this Russian love routine:

1. Deadlift

2. Parallel bar dip

Now that you have a glimpse into what is arguably The World's Most Effective exercise, let us see how you can raise your performance to the top.

In order to make this happen, I'll show you how bench press a Dodge Viper motor.

Chapter 9: How To Bench-Press A Dodge Viper Motor

500 pounds is a lot. This is the Dodge Viper's third generation V10 engine, which weighs about 500 pounds. It's a quarter of an ounce of precision engineering.

Now think about the power and strength required to lift such a heavy load. All of a sudden, 500 pounds suddenly sound very heavy, far beyond what mere mortals can lift.

However, what if you were to tell me that you have the potential to lift huge weights?

It sounds impossible. You think it is impossible?

Training for 1/4 Tons

Tony Robbins, human performance coach, did not know that the Lear 35A jet was coming to Boise. He used to weigh in at a respectable 180lbs but would soon go on to lift more than DOUBLE that amount and then continue lifting 1/4 of his iron.

Robbins was in Boise for a demonstration of a groundbreaking type of training, which is being developed by John Little's friends Peter Sisco. Robbins, a huge fan of their work wanted to interview and record their methods.

Robbins started breaking his personal weight training records quickly.

How to increase your bench strength by 277%

The bench press was at the beginning of the record-breaking session. Robbins told Sisco and Little that he only could bench 180 pounds. Sisco, Little and Robbins loaded 300 pounds onto a power-rack and invited Robbins lift the weight in his strongest range. They held it for 10 second. Robbins lifted his barbell with grace, surprise!

They increased the weight by 390 pounds and then challenged Robbins to do it again. He did it... and didn't break a sweat. Now it was 450 lbs. Robbins lifted the bar again. Astonished at the feat, Robbins asked Sisco for 500 pounds to build the bar.

What did you think happened next?

Robbins successfully loaded 1/4 ton iron onto the bar and then he rammed it up for 500 pounds.

The Ultimate Strength Workout

So how did Robbins do it? Isometrics is the secret to Robbins' ultimate strength workout. You can lift heavier weights if you do it in the strongest possible range of motion. Tony Robbins could lift the same weight as a Dodge Viper with a zero range in motion and increase his bench press by 277% in a single session.

This means that you could perform a strong-range bench pressing of 250-400 lbs if your bench press is capable of supporting 200 pounds. You might be surprised to find that 1/4 ton is not so heavy.

Next we'll reveal the origins of the ultimate strength workout and show you how it can help.

Chapter 10: Starr Man

It's not something that is used that often anymore, but it was there in the past. Get into a time machine and go back to the 60s. It was a different world.

The Mini skirt and The Beatles era, isometric exercises were sweeping the globe and helping athletes smash records. Ordinary Joes built Superman physiques. Indeed, many considered this new lifting trend revolutionary.

A young man at the time would have remarkable success with this system. He would then go on to be the author of one of the most highly acclaimed books ever written on strength training. His name? Bill Starr.

When You Wish Upon Starr

Starr was an iconic 7-stone weakling years before his novel The Strongest Shall Save Survive. With a modest 130 pound weight, he graduated high school and aspired to play college sports.

Starr realized he would need to transform his physique to compete against the big boys on campus and joined the Air Force. The US soldier would see nine years of active service before he realized his dream. Starr, then 27, enrolled at Southern Methodist University. He tried out for the American football team.

Starr fulfilled his wish. Starr was an average sports jock trying to gain an advantage over the opposition. Starr realized his chance and knew the incredible success of the system, so he began to push, pull and press his way to greatness.

Psychological Edge

Starr did his training in the following way: Starr learned that the university had placed ten isometric racks underneath the stadium. Starr would then use one of these racks or the York Barbell Company's Isometric Courses. Starr waited until the football players had finished before scaling the barrier to access the racks. After he was safe inside, Starr hid in the shadows of the nightwatchman to perform his sessions in the darkness.

His efforts paid off.

Starr, despite his small stature, would soon be able to play right-guard and set a national powerlifting world record in 1968. Following a stint as assistant editor at Strength and Health, he would become the Baltimore Colts conditioning coach and help them achieve Super Bowl success.

Starr shares his thoughts about strength. "If you believe you're more powerful, you can have a psychological edge on your opponent regardless of whether they are in front of you, underneath them, opposite them, or on top of you on a wrestling mat. Athletes who are strong have great confidence.

Record Breaking

With the psychological edge and confidence gained from the adoption of the isometrics system, athletes were able to make amazing progress in many sports.

* Indiana University was ranked number one in swimming. Jim Counsilman became a coach for his students and they soon set national and global records. Encouraged by these amazing results, all the swimming coaches in the country soon followed their lead and quickly installed isometrics racks.

* Jim Beatty won the indoor mile in track and cross-country after having done isometrics. Jay Sylvester also broke the record three times in the discussion.

Bill March, a competitor in weightlifting would be the one to watch. He won all the prizes with his fast lifts. In 1963 Philadelphia Open, it was almost predictable that a world record was established and another champion won gold.

This is impressive reading. Bruce Lee, movie star, certainly believed that. Joe Weider, a bodybuilding expert, described Lee's physique as "the best I have ever seen". Lee would quickly adapt the system to his own exercises.

Get ready to test drive this innovative system in the next chapters.

Chapter 11: Ultimate Strength Exercise

"Even though you may not be interested in using itos in a program of your own, learn how to use them so that others can benefit from your knowledge. It's the ultimate strength exercise, and it's at danger of being lost. This can't be allowed."

-- Bill Starr

Learning isometrics takes little effort. Your reward? Increase muscle mass and strength in less time.

There is however one drawback to pure isometrics. The system is simple, but it is very difficult to accurately determine if you put 100% effort.

This problem can also be solved easily. This was also discussed in our earlier story about Tony Robbins and his Dodge Viper engine. What is it? It is a way to make the weight move a few extra inches.

Isotonics

Bill Starr called these isotonic isometrics. He found that moving the bars a short distance before lockout was significantly more productive then pure isometric contractions. It removed the uncertainty about whether or not the bar actually moved. It also allows you to track your progress throughout the week.

Tony Robbins would have no way of measuring his strength with the bench press if he didn't have these small isotonic movement. But he has now got tangible proof and easy to track numbers.

The increased involvement of your nervous system is another benefit. Due to these demands, it takes more time to recover than isometrics. This is something to consider when training.

Before we go through the protocol in detail, I would like to give this warning advice:

* The best way for this system to be integrated into your workout routine is to do just a few exercises at first. As with all forms of strength training there is a learning curve. Over time you will gain more proficiency and be better equipped to use them. You should be patient and not rush.

* Make sure to warm your muscles up properly. Why is this important? A partial-range of motion will allow you to lift heavier weights than you would if you were lifting them in a traditional way. Robbins' bench was boosted by 277%. Similar increases are possible.

* If you're incorporating the system into your routine, then practice your Isotonic contractions during your workout. Bill

Starr would have to scale the wire fence of his university in order to do his isotonic exercise on non-lifting days. You can also use this protocol for your own personal training.

I now know what isotonics means. Let me walk you through it and teach you what you need.

Chapter 12: Isometrics Explained

There will be some awkwardness if you haven't lifted weights before, or performed the strength-training exercises mentioned in these pages. But don't worry. This is completely normal.

And for anyone who is unfamiliar with some or all of the exercises I cover, I just want to tell you that bodybuilding.com provides a terrific collection of videos you can access at http://www.bodybuilding.com/exercises.

You can learn weight lifting exercises by doing them yourself, rather than just reading books. Check out these exercises before you decide to make a move.

Equipment for Weight Training

The following guide is based on the assumption that you have access free-loading barsbells, plenty of plates, sturdy bench or power racks, lots and lots of plates, strong benches, parallel bars free for dips, an overhead pulley/chin up bar, and free standing parallel bars.

Even if all you have is a barbell, bench, and stands, it's possible to transform yourself. These items alone will provide enough for your primary needs of pushing, pulling, and squatting.

1/4 Ton Bench Press

Since everyone is familiarity with the bench press we will use this exercise for our isometrics examples. Because you will only be training in your strongest motion range (the last few inch), you will be able and able to lift significantly higher weights than normal. It is important to always have a backup plan, such as a partner or power rack.

How much iron will you be able to lift? It is normal to see a 25-50% increase in iron, with some cases even greater.

Breathing

There are two camps of thought on the topic of breathing. Pete Sisco recommends that you inhale through your mouth as you push the bar into its hold position. I know of other practitioners who use this method, and I see the merits. I would recommend Bill Starr's way of breathing, which is slightly different, for the moment.

The rule of thumb is to hold your breath for the duration if you are experiencing an isometric contraction. Why is this? The reason is that if you take in too much air, your ability of applying maximum force to the lift will be diminished. To help you get the most out of your lift, take deep breaths and fill up your lungs.

The Push

This is where the fun begins. This is where your potential strengths and limits can be explored.

After a thorough warm up, lower the pins of the power rack to three-to-four inch below the farthest point of your reach. Now take hold of the bar, and exhale deeply. Now push.

Your bar will rise smoothly if you were careful and did not add too much weight. Now, hold the bar one inch under lock-out. Keep your elbows straight and don't extend your arms beyond the point where lock-out is reached. You will transfer tension to your joints. Remember that we want the muscles to contract.

How long will you hold on to this position?

The exercise should take between 6-12 seconds. If you have trouble keeping your hand on the bar for six seconds or more, lower your weight by 20%. For those who can manage 12 seconds or more, increase your lift 10%. You can slowly lower your bar to the pins when you feel weak.

Advanced Technique

This system can also be used in lifts to strengthen your weakest muscles. The push from the chest is usually the most difficult part of this move.

Here's what to do:

You can place the pins on the rack just above the chest area in the bench press. Next, perform your isotonic contractions for 6-12 second intervals.

This advanced technique may also be used to help with "sticking spots" in certain exercises. For example, the middle third of the biceps curl would be used.

Iso Tips

* To be effective in isometrics and isotonics, you must have a high level of concentration. Focus solely on your form, and the muscles being exercised.

* This is an excellent way to fit in a workout even if you have limited time. Combine any push, pull, or squat movement with this system and your body will be on the fast track for impressive gains.

* Work to strengthen the weakest parts of your exercise program. If you do this, you will continue to make progress in all aspects of your training.

Tips for Workouts

You can decide how you organize your workouts. You can practice your isometrics exercise on non-training days. Or you can move them into your routine at the end of your day and do your "holds" there.

The choice of exercises you choose is simple. Avoid isolation exercises such biceps curls, leg extension and the like. Instead, put your focus on the simple and powerful core bodybuilding moves. Why?

Because they enable you to take on the heaviest of weights and offer the most bang for the buck when it comes to bodybuilding.

Only three moves can provide you with the artillery firepower necessary to achieve great gains. What are these moves? You can push, pull or squat. To strengthen your upper body, look no further then the dip, bench press and pulldown/row. Your lower body can be taken care of by a variety of squats, sometimes substituting for the deadlift.

You don't have to be complicated. Rotate these movements and you can effectively target all major muscles groups. Your reward? You'll get more strength and a stronger body.

Performance

As always, you should perform your isos within the strongest range and in the final third of an exercce. This allows you to keep your holds within the last few inches of each move, while avoiding lockout. (This is when your arms and legs are at their most extended.

Next we'll tackle problematic waistlines.

Chapter 13: Bruce Lee Abs

With a loss of employment of approximately PS6 billion due to back pain in the UK, it is estimated that around 180 million working hours are lost each year. But despite these alarming numbers, a pain in the lower back can easily be treated.

The common solution to this problem is to strengthen your core muscles. And how can we do that? We do crunches, leg raises, and sit ups. However, if you continue to do these exercises as directed, you will soon feel the gnawing pain in the lower regions of the back. It is similar to the worst kind of toothache.

Why is this? The truth is that there is a lot misinformation around about the best stomach exercises. Unfortunately, many of the core training and six-pack regimens often fed to trainees in gyms or health clubs fall into this category.

Is there an option? Is there an alternative to putting our delicate lower backs in danger? There is. The following safe, simple, and quick stomach exercises will help you get rid of the monotony of sit-ups, leg raises, crunches, and sit-ups.

Stomach Vacuum Exercise

Most likely, you don't know much about the stomach vacuum exercise. But this isometrics exercise was a key part of Bruce Lee's stomach training. It will flatten the stomach better than a thousand hard crunches. Before I explain how to do them, let me tell you about their purpose.

Picture a woman's narrow-waisted Corset to get a better understanding of their function. These figure-hugging clothes were used to torture women in Victorian times. Imagine that the corset lacings are being pulled tight to pull the abdomen in. As you do so, your stomach will begin to shrink and disappear. Sounds painful? Yes! You can still achieve the same transformation by doing the stomach-vacuum exercise. It is painless and easy.

Let me first tell you, crunches will not pull in your abdomen. The six-pack muscle (rectus Abdominis), runs vertically. This is a problem since the transverse abdomen is the one you want. They are the largest of the six main abdominal muscle groups and they are composed of fibres running horizontally. It is a corset-like structure. (This is how they got their nickname, "the corset-muscle". This is why you should target these special horizontal fibres to achieve a tight and trim middle.

This is accomplished by using a combination breathing control and muscular tension. The breathing is when you empty your lungs. The muscular tension comes when you swallow your stomach. Does that sound simple? Excellent. Now let's look at this exercise.

Here's what to do:

1. Begin in a bent-over position. Place your hands on the knees. Position your feet shoulder width apart.

2. You should breathe in and out slowly three to four times. Finally, exhale fully. (This is very important as the transverse abdominal muscles must be fully contracted by full exhalation.

3. Try to forcefully sucking in your stomach while avoiding taking in any air. As an aid, imagine pulling your stomach button backwards as much as you can.

4. For 10 seconds, keep this muscle contraction going with your stomach pulled in.

5. Inhale deeply through the nose until you reach your count. Then repeat the 10th time.

The Plank Exercise

Remember that pain in the lower back? Now, I'd like to share another isometric exercise. This one works the external abdominal oblique muscles on your stomach and back. Training these core muscles will not only keep them strong and healthy but also stabilize your entire upper body.

The plank can be used as an abdominal exercise, tummy trimmer, or abdominal workout. The plank, like the stomach vacuum before, is an isometric exercise that targets your core muscles. It also strengthens your shoulders and arms. Why do these two stomach exercises complement each other so well? The stomach vacuum and plank help you build strongman strength by keeping your muscles contracted.

Ready to go? Here are your options:

1. Start by lying on one side. You should align your hips and shoulders with your legs.

2. You should rest your elbow on the ground, just below your shoulder. Your forearm should rest flat on a table, and your left arm should be spread out on your side.

3. After you are in a position, lift your hips from the ground. Be careful not to let your bottom sink. Your entire body should be straightened like a piece of wood. You must also keep your stomach muscles contracted.

4. Continue to breath in and out. Next, do the same exercise on each side.

5. Begin with a plank position and aim for 1 min. As you progress, you can either increase your time or add more sets.

Go on to the next section, and we'll be busy answering your most commonly asked questions.

Chapter 14: Frequently Asked Questions

Q: Are isometrics safe?

A: Yes, all strenuous exercise has some risk. This book explains how to perform isometric exercise. This book is a good example of how isometric exercises can be dangerous. The short answer is yes! You just need to follow the breathing, and exercise steps that I have clearly described.

It is forbidden to perform rapid and intense movements, unless you follow the guidelines. This is no different from lifting heavy weights in an uncontrolled way. The result? This can lead to injury and even a tear in your muscle. Instead, ensure you are in good form during all exercises and that you follow proper breathing.

Q: How often should you train?

A: We have one job when it comes to training effectively: We want the best possible response and the lowest effective dose. This is why Bruce Lee's principle of Tao would be a great example to us. It means you should abandon the common bodybuilding advice which recommends that you exercise for hours every day, and only train what you absolutely need.

What numbers do you need? Wolverine Strength Secrets features my thoughts on the benefits of abbreviated exercise and some easy routines that use the principle Tao. This book has two exercises for deadlifts. They are effective in building strength and size.

Q: I travel a lot. Is this a style of training that I can bring on the road?

A: Absolutely. The best thing about isometric exercises is their portability. You do not need to purchase expensive gym equipment. This means you can enjoy your training wherever you are. The best thing? It takes less time, too.

Q: Do I have to do any kind of stretching before I can try these exercises?

A: Always warm up. Pete Sisco is an expert on Isometrics and recommends you get on an exercise machine for a quick warm-up before you start lifting weights. You can add these isometric moves to your weight lifting routines without having to warm up.

Q: When's the best time to exercise.

It doesn't matter. It is important that you find the best time for you. If possible, you should eat your largest meal right after working out. This is so important. It's because the body is more responsive to nutrient synthesis and uptake after intense exercise like weight training. That's great news if you want muscle building! If you are looking to add bully steak to your physique, I suggest that you start training before your evening meal.

Q: I have heard about isometrics training before. When can I expect results?

A: The very first workout. Your posture, body and strength will improve from the first workout. You will see a rapid increase in muscle definition and firmness. You will be more resilient. These changes won't be limited to your physique. They have an impact on every area of your life.

Chapter 15: Dragons Vs Drones

Dan Kennedy, "Millionaire Maker", a serial entrepreneur. He has mentored hundreds of thousands of small business owners to grow their businesses from nothing to seven figures. Kennedy offers private consultations by phone or online for $800. So people listen to Kennedy and drop their worries.

Kennedy spoke out about fitness during an interview. I would be willing to pay more for the hour than the four. I want the end result. I don't want the time."

Did you catch the last part? Let me repeat: "I want to see the end result." I don't really need the time.

Kennedy is referring here to Occam's Razor principles and Tao. They show how it is futile to have more and what can be achieved with less. Kennedy's 1-hour fitness program instantly makes Kennedy's more appealing option than its 4-hour-long, flabby counterpart. Why? Because the millionaire entrepreneur understands how valuable time is.

Time is valuable

This is the "value of your time" which forms the foundation of all effective strength training. It is impossible to assess the effectiveness of a routine or workout without this measurement. Are you going to hunch and feel for your assessment? Is it your bar's weight? What about reps? What yardsticks do YOU use?

Pete Sisco is the author. I interviewed him about it for my website a while back (you can find my interview in a bonus chapter at the end of the book). Pete is responsible for The World's Fastest Workout. This is an extremely short method of building muscle. It's based on the same Isometric holds Bruce Lee used with great success.

Pete talked about his past training experiences in the San Fernando Valley's commercial gym. Pete, unlike John Little (his training partner), is a busy guy and doesn't like spending too much time in the gym.

Pete records everything so that you can be sure. Every exercise, weight and rep is documented. Pete does something that no one else in the gym is doing. Is it possible to guess? He counts everything on his wristwatch. Every second.

Why? Pete Sisco understands time, just as Dan Kennedy.

Pete was measuring training intensity in the same manner Kennedy was using time as a measure of a training program's efficiency.

Both of them understand the principle Tao. They both know the Ninja Dragon

Star as well as Occam's Razor's cutthroat blade.

Bruce Lee knew it too. He realized the true value of time when he was searching for a workout that suited his philosophy of achieving optimal results while consuming the least energy.

Dragon Heart

So, what now? Wolverine Strength Secrets is my essay on wolverines. In it, I compare them to their coddled poodle counterparts. I also offered a challenge asking, "Which one are yours?"

Ninja Strength Secrets allows me to take that challenge one more step. How? You are invited to accept a new challenge.

Here's how it works:

Drones, which are male honeybees, are found in nature. They live in colonies and can't sting. Their only function in life is to mate for the queen bee.

Drones can be described as lazy workers or 'idlers' in the human realm. They are lazy and live off others, doing tedious or menial tasks. Their lives are boring and monotonous.

Dragons don't live in colonies. Dragons live free. While they are not able to sting or make honey they can have lions' claws, the tails and breath fire.

Dragons are fiercely alert, dangerous and formidable -- they aren't lazy and don't live off the help of others. Their life is exciting and thrilling, not like the drone.

They have a dragon heart.

Let me ask you: Which one?

I challenge you, gentle reader, to find out. Wishing you luck on your journey.

Chapter 16: Keeping The Dream Alive

I hope you found isometrics useful. Bill Starr was right to say that they were the ultimate strength workout. We must not allow them to get lost. They're worth the effort, so I encourage you to give them another try.

Isometrics can be a simple way to gain strength, shape your body like Bruce Lee's martial arts master Bruce Lee. And it takes very little time.

Include them in your weightlifting routine. Get better at it. Next, share your knowledge with others to help keep this system of strength alive.

Hong Kong

As one walks along Avenue of Stars near Tsim Shi Tsui in Hong Kong one is greeted at the water's edge by a 2.5-meter bronze statue of Bruce Lee. He's in his classic ready to strike pose from the 1972 movie

Fist of Fury. Bruce Lee was more to Hong Kong than a movie star. He was also its national hero and ambassador. His movies helped Hong Kong's movie industry reach new heights in the realm of motion pictures. His movies introduced the world to the culture of Hong Kong. His films were what made Hong Kong stand out as a modern country.

Hong Kong or The Fragrant Harbour in Chinese is an independent region on the Pearl River Delta of East Asia. To its north is the Chinese province Guangdong, while Macau lies to its west. It boasts a total land surface of 1,106 kilometres and more that 7.3 millions inhabitants from different nationalities. It is also the fourth most densely populated territory or autonomous state.

After the First Opium War (1839), Hong Kong was an British colony. In 1839, the island of Hong Kong was charted and named by the Kowloon Peninsula. It was then followed by a 99 years lease of New Territories, which was signed between British and Hong Kong administrations starting in 1898. After World War II, Japan captured Hong Kong and then allied forces recaptured it in 1945. In the 1980s, talks took place between China's United Kingdom and Britain. This led to the 1984 Sino-British Joint Declaration. This declaration opened the way to the handover of Hong Kong's control in 1997. The SAR was a special administrative region with high autonomy under People's Republic of China.

In the 1970s the country went through several reforms that changed its future. Murray MacLehose, the nation's longest-serving governor and reform-minded governor, governed the country for the majority of the decade. He was a reformer in every aspect of the country's economic life. It evolved from a manufacturing centre to become a financial hub. The market started to gravitate towards franchises and business.

During this time, the culture of the country also experienced major changes. It became a blend of eastern and western ideas. It was able to preserve many Chinese traditions while also experiencing a baptism of Western culture.

However, before 1970s reforms, the country was still in poverty. Bruce Lee was living in Hong Kong's dirty streets when he was a young boy. He grew up in Hong Kong, a city choked by narrow streets, Lorries. Taxies. Pushcarts. Neon signs. One side of the city was filled with exotic smells, while the other had a strong stench of sludge.

Bruce Lee spent most his childhood fighting, hiding from the world, playing, and having fun in Hong Kong's narrow, dark and filthy streets.

Early Days

Bruce Lee's parents, American immigrants, returned to Honk Kong a few weeks after his birth. Bruce Lee's sudden climate change caught him off guard. He had difficulty adapting to the humid climate in his country. Soon he began to feel sick and he was diagnosed with a chronic illness. Through his childhood, he was always underweight due to prolonged illness.

Bruce Lee lived with the family in a large apartment on Nathan Road, but he was unable to enjoy this luxury for too long. Bruce's elder brother and father, was killed by his uncle. Bruce's father assumed responsibility for looking after his brother's family. The apartment was shared by about 20 people, many of whom were accompanied by their pets (cats, dogs, hens, etc.). Bobby, an Alsatian Dog named Bobby, was his favorite among all of his family members.

It would be wrong for Bruce Lee to claim that he came from an impoverished background. His father was an investor in real estate and had many assets throughout Hong Kong. This enabled him to collect large amounts of property rent. In addition, he made a lot from his concerts and shows. Lees could easily have a lavish lifestyle, if he had the rent money and the income his father earned from shows. Bruce says that his father was a'miser.' However, his father was a kind and generous man who always helped his family. His father paid many times the medical bills for his friends, who otherwise couldn't afford them.

He often accompanied his dad to his shows. Bruce became friends with Siukee Lun, who he affectionally called a unicorn, during one of his shows. Siu's grandfather, Bruce's father and actor in Chinese opera, was also Siu. The three-year difference in age between the boys was not a problem for Bruce, who lost no fight against Unicorn. He loved fighting.

His father was very annoyed at his son's tendency to pick up fights over other children. As a punishment, he didn't seem to notice that breaking sticks was an option. However, this practice led to a split between the father & son.

His mother was his favourite of the two parents. His school fees were paid and he was dealt with by his teacher complaints. His teachers frequently told her that he didn't attend school regularly. He was known to skip class in order to hang out with his street friends. His mother said that Bruce had never changed his personality. Bruce was known for his habit of going to the streets with his friends and he often did this. 'A movie star', young Bruce replied.

From an early age, Bruce displayed the characteristics of generosity and compassion that he learned from father. On a sunny day, Bruce ran quickly out of the house naked. As she followed Bruce out of the house, she saw him assist a blind man crossing the street. Grace Lee was very proud of the moment.

The children called him "little dragon", while the elders called him "MoSi Tung", which is an acronym that means "never sits down." He would often read in his bed at night. His mother says that this is probably the reason he became nearsighted. Bruce was six when he developed nearsightedness and needed glasses.

Young Bruce loved to play pranks on siblings and his friends. It was his tendency to play pranks upon others that his friends most disliked about him. He was known to go over the line many times. One example was pushing his sister Phoebe into a swimming pool. She nearly drowned. She held his head in the water until it was clear. He promised never to play such a prank again. Bruce has not been to the swimming pool since that fateful day.

Bruce attended La Salle at the age 12 for his senior secondary education. It was a Christian missionary schools. Most of the students were Chinese Catholics. From the first day, he began to draw attention to himself and his classmates for the wrong reasons. Although he was considered a "tough pupil" by all his teachers, Brother Henry was an ounce of hope. He was the one teacher who understood that Bruce's energy needed to be directed in a constructive way. He hired him to clean the board, run errands and other tasks. Bruce did as he requested.

Bruce loved to read, but he was not interested in school. But he didn't care much for history or art. He hated biology.

Years of British colonial persecution had engendered malice in the hearts the Hong Kong's free and young generation towards their oppressor. They grew to hear the stories of the English atrocities against their ancestors. There were many anti-Britain movements in Hong Kong. Such groups encouraged hatred of British citizens in Hong Kong. Bruce Lee was the leader one such gang at his school. They often went to King George V School, where they studied British children, in order to show their anger and hatred of the British. Bruce and his gang threatened to throw abuses and even stones at them, hoping to incite them into fighting. They would then climb the fence of the school to mock the children who were playing in the school's playground, if all their efforts were unsuccessful. The gang often succeeded in starting a fight, but they never won the fight. Bruce and his gang had a lot more pupils at King George V School than their King George V School classmates. Police were frequently called in to stop the fight. His father had the most to apologize to police for his son's juvenile acts. Bruce was beaten repeatedly at home. When he came home with a blackeye, he would speak to no one and then run straight to his room, hoping his father wouldn't notice or that his mom would tell his father. She sometimes did.

A child fears an absent father more than an angry dad. Bruce's growing years saw a lot of his father not being home to vent his anger. The two mechanisms a child uses to cope with the absence from his father are either depressive or positive. Either it becomes depressed, or it decides to become more successful that its father. Bruce chose to do the latter. Bruce's father was a successful actor and a martial artist. Bruce resolved in his heart that he would be a bigger, more successful actor than his father. As history recalls, he beat his father in this domain.

Rise of an Actor

Bruce Lee began his love affair with the world cinema at three months of age. He was the baby carried by his father during one scene in the movie 'Golden Gate Girl. Six years ago, he was cast in the movie 'The Birth of Mankind. He plays the role of a child who fights with Unicorn. Chow Sui, one of the most popular Cantonese television shows of the time, was his first major part. He played the part of a wise boy who worked at a Hong Kong factory. Lee Siu Lung (The little dragon) was his role.

He was primarily an orphan or street urchin in his early roles. In his later years, he became a juvenile rebel or derelict. Many of those movies featured fight scenes. His own style of fighting was already established with trademark moves like the slow gaze, the thumb wiping across the nose, and the admonishing hand. His father gave him formal training in "t'aichi", which is street fighting art. He was proficient at incorporating 't'aichi' movements into his fight scenes, and he did so many times. He appeared in more than twenty films as a young actor. His most memorable role was that of Orphan, where he played his only child actor lead role. Through every role, he was able to grow tremendously as an actor.

China was the first country to introduce motion pictures. The first Chinese movie, titled 'The Battle of Dingjunshan', was released in theatres in China in the years

1896 and 1905. Shanghai was the centre of China's film industry in the early decades. The "golden period" of Chinese film production is believed to have been 1930. In 1931, following the Japanese invasion and occupation of China, the film industry was severely curtailed. Filmmakers fled to Hong Kong and Chongqing. After the shift from Shanghai to Hong Kong, most movies were set in the western suburbs of Hong Kong and Shanghai. No attempt was made to capture the reality of life on the mainland. Many martial art movies used special effects to make the scene more realistic. For example, the protagonist could do fifty somersaults in air or leap over hundred meters from one place to another. The film Wong Fei Hung was born between 1847-1924. This film focuses on his life as a master of martial arts. Wong was an instructor of the Hung Gar style, or 'Kung Fu,' and also practiced herbal medicine.

Hu Peng directed the film. Hu Peng insisted on not using special effects to fight sequences. He preferred to see real fighting scenes in movies. It was the first experience that the audience saw a true fighting scene without special effects.

Kwan Tak Hing, Bruce's friend, played Wong Fei Hung's character in the movie. Kwan Tak Hing, just like Bruce's dad, was a trained martial artist. Much like Bruce, he was skilled in Hung Gar Kung Fu. He had also learned the Shaolin style fighting, which is based around the moves of animals. His movies were based around the philosophy of Martial Virtue'. His films and young Bruce were greatly influenced. His films were a huge success at the boxoffice, earning him a huge fan base, which included Bruce Lee. Bruce could quote every dialogue in every film that he made during this time.

Kung Fu

Kung Fu can be translated as work-man. This refers to someone who uses art to exercise their body. The expression 'Kung Fu, or labor, has the same meaning as the word Congou' in the south, which is applied to a certain type of tea. It is applied medically in China to the exact same subjects as the German Heil Gymnastik (or curative gymnastics), and the French Kinesiologie (or science relating to movement)

(Extra from John Dudgeon's 'Kung Fu' book.

Hong Kong's 1950s were plagued by anarchy and crippling economic growth, extreme poverty, and overpopulation. Many people fled communist China for safety and refuge in Hong Kong. The education provided by the state was only for a select few. Many others wandered aimlessly in search of work in cities that were not well-off. This led to a large number youth on the streets who, in search for easy money and cheap adventure, created gangs. All over Hong Kong, there were numerous gangs which fought each other for control over different areas. Gang wars were commonplace on the streets. Many of them led to bloody fights. The members of these gangs did not have access to weapons so they only engaged in hand-to hand combat. Bruce, despite his admission to a private high school, was always drawn to the streets. He founded his own small gang and gave it the name "Tigers at Junction Street".

Bruce met William Cheung the first and only time he was present at a birthday party. William Cheung, a street fighter of Hong Kong fame, was the most prominent. Wing Chun was his preferred style of Kung Fu. Bruce approached Bruce at the party and asked him if he could teach him.

William declined to take him seriously, and instead suggested that he focus on his acting career.

Bruce was badly beat in a fight with gang members one day and demanded to learn a martial art. Although Bruce had received formal training from his father in 'tai Chi', the slow moves of taichi were useless to him. He wanted to learn fast moves, those with intensity and strength. After constant pestering, his mother finally gave in to his request for money.

After getting money from the mother, he sought out William Cheung and demanded that he be trained at his school. William refused to let him go to the Restaurant Workers Union Hall because he had solicited so long. He introduced him then to Yip Man who was the mastermind of the school. Yip Man was influenced by Bruce's celebrity status and he happily agreed to take Bruce in.

Bruce dedicated his whole life to Wing Chun once he had started training. This devotion quickly became an obsession. His obsession soon turned into a passion. Bruce was beginning to master the Wing Chun style Kung Fu.

Kung Fu is often used in the umbrella of many Chinese martial arts. It does not only refer to the history of martial arts, but also any skill or achievement that is a result of hard work. Kung Fu is a term that can be used for any ability that was acquired in this manner. It does not have to be restricted to the martial arts. Kung Fu is used extensively to identify a notable share of the Chinese Martial Arts in the modern world. In this sense, Kung Fu is typical for highly varied martial structures that are difficult to trace. This makes the Chinese arts stand out from the other popular categories of martial arts.

Martial arts were established in China almost for the same reasons it had in other societies: To help with hunting activities and defend oneself from the enemies. Other than this, martial techniques including those related to weaponries and militaries can be traced back thousands of year in China's past history. The solemnization of the arts was initiated by the Yellow Emperor Huangdi who ruled China in 2698 B.C. History claims that he also invented a way to fight for the army. It was fought with horned headgear called Jiao Di (or Horn Butting). It evolved to include strikes, joint locks and blocks. The Qin Dynasty (approximately 221, B.C.) made it a popular sport.).

It is also important that you understand that Chinese martial art has a longstanding spiritual and philosophical meaning within Chinese culture. The Zhou Dynasty (1045 B.C. to 256 B.C.) saw martial arts grow along with ideas like Confucianism or Taoism. They were not in isolation from them. For example, the Taoist concept of Ying-Yang (the universal contraries) was linked in a large measure to the hard-and-soft methods that make up Kung Fu. The models of Confucianism were used to develop the art, which was based on the ideal practices that must be followed.

Kung Fu is a way to speak about Buddhism. Buddhism originated in India, and was brought to China by the close relationship that existed between the two countries during the period 58-76 A.D. The monks who traveled between China and India to spread Buddhism was in agreement with this. Bodhidharma an Indian is the most frequently cited figure in the history of martial art. Bodhidharma preached at the Shaolin Temples, China recently built. His ideas of self-effacement and control helped to transform their thinking.

Although this idea is a little skewed, it appears that Bodhidharma arrived in China and the monks quickly became famous martial artists experts. They worked tirelessly at their craft. At the same time, various styles of Kung Fu were being taught by the Taoist monasteries.

KungFu used to be an exclusive art, and was only taught by the rulers at the time. Due to Japanese occupations and subsequent invasions from the French and British, the Chinese encouraged martial arts experts to open up their doors and to teach the art form to the people in order to exterminate foreign invaders. Unfortunately, the masses soon learned that the martial arts couldn't withstand the bullets fired by their enemies.

Kung Fu faced a new enemy in the face Communism several years later. Mao Zedong took control of China's government and tried to abolish all things that were customary to build his version of Communism. Kung Fu books as well as Chinese history, including the majority of literature on the Shaolin Temple art, were subject to attack during his rule. A number of Kung Fu teachers fled to China, where they were able to teach the martial arts. This was a result of communist rule.

Bruce was skilled in Wing Chun out of a wide range of martial arts. Wing Chun is the name for a martial art that was developed in southern China approximately 300 years ago. Ng Mui the Buddhist holy sibling, was the original inventor. She was a Shaolin Kung Fu teacher and created a way to get rid of the inherent weakness of other Shaolin structures. This new system was closely guarded, and it was only passed on to a select few students. This style, known as Wing Chun after Ng Mui's initial student, Yim Wing Chun (also known as Yim Wing Chun), became well-known over time. Yip Man, the grandmaster of Wing Chun contemporary, brought the style from China into Hong Kong, and then to the rest.

Wing Chun is based on the principle that the shortest distance between points can be measured along a straightline. Wing Chun kicks are quicker than t'ai Chi's larger cirlcles.

Wing Chun moves aim to get the enemy on the straightest possible path. This is because the shortest distance between any two points can be a straight line. The central line, an imaginary perpendicular arc that intersects with the opponent's vital body organs (throat, stomach, stomach, and even groin), is the principal target. Wing Chun knocks should be carried centrally, rather than obliquely from one's shoulders, like in other martial arts. This technique helps to understand the central concept of Kung Fu. While in other martial arts forms, the punch can be made obliquely by moving from the shoulder towards the centerline. The reason is that the distance is shorter if one moves the hand from the shoulder towards the centerline of the opponent's chest.

Wing Chun's most essential aspect is the concept 'chi' or'sticking hands'. Wing Chun is performed by two specialists who keep contact with one other's forearms during the execution of the techniques. This allows them to prepare each other to detect changes and change in the body's mechanics, force, thrust, and 'touch'. This practice increases compassion, which allows an expert to accurately attack and stand the actions of an opponent. Chi jerk is also known as "sticking feet" and consists of predetermined leg-centered movements that are executed in a manner similar to Chi Sao.

There are three stages to Chi Sao Training. Each stage requires that practitioners move from the predefined moves into random moves. Finally, at the advanced stage, they must practice blindfolded. It is important to remember that although the moves of Chi Sao do not apply in combat situations, they are useful for developing coordination and awareness, which are essential aspects of martial arts. Bruce Lee first experienced the interacting forces with Yin Yang through Chi Sao.

The philosophy of Yin-Yang is derived from the age-old reflection on nature. It labels the way all things in the universe naturally group themselves into the pairs of contraries - sun and moon and winter and summer,heaven & earth, up & down, male / female, inside & outside, activity and inactivity.

These words are from the section called 'appended remarks' found in the Chinese classic text I Ching. These two schools have the idea of Yin and Yang. Two conflicting but equally compensating modules create harmony.

The philosophy Yin-Yang explains why nature creates a third energy. This energy diffuses throughout the universe and becomes a vital force for all living creatures. The roots of the philosophy are found in many Chinese traditional religions, primarily Taoism (and Confucianism). Ch'i can literally mean "air" (or "breath"), but it is a concept that refers to energy flow or the life force that permeates the universe. But, the Chinese have debated the notion of "ch'i" for centuries. Some Chinese philosophers believe it's a separate force, while others think it's part of the physical universe.

Bruce, having just returned from school, ran straight for Yip Man's class. The delight of passersby was evident as he practiced and attempted new moves while on his way. He didn't stop home, either. He continued practicing the moves he learned in the class until he was finally put to bed by his mother.

Yip Man was told one day by his older classmates that Bruce Lee easily defeated them in the fights. They were very angry about this. They believed that he was teaching them something they didn't understand. They wanted to be taught the exact same things that Bruce was teaching them. Yip Man soon realized that Bruce Lee was serious in Kung Fu and had a bright future.

Moving to America

A year after learning Kung Fu, he began to take an interest dancing. He began learning cha cha cha at a local dance school. He used to visit the school along with Victor Kan who was a Wing Chun student. Bruce first learned to dance in order impress Pearl Cho, his girlfriend.

Amy Chan became his first significant girlfriend. Later, he was known as Pak Yan in the Eastern film world. They often went dancing to the local club. Bruce dressed up for Amy's dates in sharp clothes. He ironed his own clothes. She loved him for being funny and kind. He became difficult to control when he was around other people.

Bruce was experiencing more difficulties controlling his emotions, such as anger and frustration, as he grew older. He was also struggling to understand the subtleties, nuances, and details of Chi Sao. It was a very difficult period in his life. He was frequently involved in fights against other gangs. He did not carry weapons such as a knife or blade. Most of his fights involved him breaking his nose and kicking and punching other people. Nearly all of the fights involved his mother visiting a police station to rescue her son.

William Cheung struck his opponent in a gang fight so severely that William Cheung's mother and her son had to rush down the street to rescue him. Hotheadedness may be partly responsible for his inability to handle the situation. YipMan, his master, also took part in the problem by asking his pupils to perform their moves on the real world. Yip Man also encouraged patience and calmness in his students, two qualities Bruce was never able attain. Bruce never accepted defeats, even if they did come once in awhile.

Yip Man gave Bruce the advice to stop training for awhile and to look within himself. Bruce gave up his pursuit of meaningless wanderings and quit training. He used the free time to ask himself important questions such as "Why this type?" or "Why Kung Fu?". After a while, Bruce stopped searching for answers and returned to his favorite sport, Kung Fu.

Because of his quick success, many of his younger students used the knowledge of his German ancestry to protest his expulsion from school. They wanted to expel Yip man from the school. Yip Men refused to let them out. Bruce was getting tired of the hostility and he decided it was time to stop training with YipMan. Wong Sheung Leung became his mentor and then he trained with William Cheung. Wong Sheung had only a few students who he taught. Bruce frequently falsely claimed that the class was cancelled to make sure he had all of Wong Sheung's attention and time.

Brother Edward, one his teachers, encouraged him at St Francis Xavier high school to participate in 1958 interschool boxing champions. He gladly agreed to compete in the championship and trained with William Cheung. He easily passed the preliminary rounds beating his opponents by less than three rounds. In the finals, he faced Gary Elms from England, the three-time champion. His hopes and dreams were weighing heavily on his shoulders. He was beaten up by his boxing rivals who were more traditional. He was able later to block his opponent's blows with the Wing Chun technique and, using the same techniques, he defeated his opponent in the third round.

He lived a life that was dominated by street fighting and championships. The number of visits to the police station increased only. His school was barely able to support him and he often required the students to do their homework. His mother worried about her son's fate soon. The family decided to send him off to America. Bruce was hesitant to move to the States. However, his parents insisted and he couldn't refuse. His mother believed her son would only be able to have a secure life in the United States.

Hawkins Cheung (the son of William Cheung) was told by him his decision to go to the United States. He stated that his father wasn't fond of him and his family didn't respect his decision and that he had earned some respect for his own self. He stated that although his family wanted to see him become a dentist, he prefers to teach Kung Fu. Hawkins reminded Hawkins of the fact that he didn't know Wing Chun until the second version. He was missing what they called the "showy moves" in martial arts. Bruce understood what he said and decided to learn some more'showy moves before he left for the States. He was able to locate Uncle Siu who taught Kung Fu in the northern style. They agreed to a partnership. Uncle Siu would show Bruce two forms of northern Kung Fu, and he would also teach him dancing lessons. To the dismay of Uncle Siu Bruce learned the moves in only three days, contrary to his expectation of three week. At this point, he had only learned the basic steps to cha cha.

Unicorn remained Bruce's friend throughout his youth. They both enjoyed watching movies together as children. Unicorn is now an actor in the movie industry. Bruce was offered a role by the film production that had signed him to their next venture. Bruce was dissatisfied with his parents when they discussed the possibility of Bruce returning to the film industry. His parents told him that the future of their son was in the United

States. He said no to the offer with a heavy soul.

He had to get clearance from the local police in order to travel to the United States. Bruce's and Hawkins names were on the list. To be able to leave, he had his name removed from that list. He tried his best to get his name off the list, but it was not possible. The police finally caught up with William Cheung, who then bribed them to get Bruce and his son's names removed from the lists so his son could travel to Australia and Bruce can go to America.

Bruce stayed for enough time to be Crown Colony Cha ChaChampion, 1958. After saying goodbye to Unicorn, Bruce left the country for America in the next year. His mother took about 100 dollars from him and his dad another fifteen. After saying farewell to his family, he embarked on a three-week sailing across the Pacific from

San Francisco to San Francisco, California on April 9. He was not able to travel in the third class because he was given dancing lessons by first class passengers. He thought only once throughout the trip that he would have to make a decision about his future.

Uncle Sam's S: Ground for Finding Common Ground

Bruce returned to San Francisco eighteen years later. He was forced to live with his father's friend. Meanwhile, he struggled for a way of earning a living. He was able to teach dancing at the local club, and earn enough money to get by the week. He sometimes gave a quick demonstration of Kung Fu at the club. He attracted many eyes, including one from the younger brother to the owner of the local Karate School. Bruce did not have the opportunity to see San Francisco and bask in his new popularity. He received a note from his mother asking him for permission to move to Seattle, where he could stay at Chow Ping (his father's friend).

Peter, his brother on the way to joining the University of Wisconsin was with him in his final days at San Francisco. Peter occasionally saw his brother kick, punch, and babble in his sleep. His inner conflict would often take hold of him while he slept. Bruce moved from Peter to the University of Wisconsin shortly thereafter. He went on to Chow Ping's in Seattle.

Chow Ping worked back in Hong Kong for Bruce's father as a Cantonese Opera Company performer. Anguished by a serious illness, he felt the need to be in New York for the Second World War. Ruby Chow was his nurse at the local hospital where he first met Ruby Chow. After their union, the couple moved to Seattle.

Ruby Chow was also known as the "Iron Lady" among the neighbors. She fought against all the social and cultural norms to earn the title. She was well known for her bold lifestyle choices. After divorce, Chow Ping was forced to marry Chow Ping. Her community was not happy with her decision to open the first Chinese restaurant located outside Seattle's Chinatown. But her restaurant became very popular in the city's upper circle. She frequently assisted immigrants from China or Hong Kong with lodging, papers and other necessities. They were given free labor in return for working at her restaurant. Bruce was no different than any other immigrant. Chow Ping, his uncle, was expecting him to stay with him as a guest.

After being confronted by the truth, it was difficult for him to grasp the concept for the first few day. He found his name on a work schedule for only the second time in his entire life. He was given a dirty cell just like the other workers and put to work as a waiter in the restaurant. He was still able to pick up a fair amount of fights with his coworkers and customers. Ruby Chow was not pleased with him either.

The two of them often came face to face, accusing each others of disrespect and exploitation. The two of them were determined to stay together. It was as if the two of them were looking into each other's reflection in the mirror.

He worked in the evenings and studied during the day. His mother gave him some money on occasion. In addition, he worked part-time distributing leaflets to the newspapers. He enrolled at Edison Technical High School after he had enough saved. Remember, these were the days when education was heavily state funded in the United States.

He did not give up Wing Chun in spite of the struggles and chaos in life. He purchased a Wing Chun wooden stool from Hong Kong. Edison College asked Bruce Lee, who was then a student at Edison College, to give a Kung Fu demonstration. This was in 1960, the Seattle's annual 'Asian Culture Day. James DeMile (a former Heavyweight boxing champion of the US Air force and a street fighter) was sitting in the crowd. Bruce spoke to the crowd about the long-hidden secret of Chinese culture, which he was to share that day. DeMile then looked at him and said, 'You look like someone who can fight. You might consider coming up to me.

Bruce smiled as DeMile looked at Bruce, his shorter opponent of 5'7 inches and 140-pounds. Bruce then invited him for an attack. DeMile tried to hit Bruce with heavy blows on the jaw. Bruce was amazed to find that he was able defend himself from the punch. He blocked it with his wrist. DeMile tried many other moves in his book but was stopped by Bruce. DeMile was left helpless as he stood before Bruce. He then swiftly moved DeMile's wrist in a unique way, only to come to a halt before his face. DeMile asked Bruce to teach him some of his moves as the crowd cheered Bruce. Jesse Glover, an African American Judophile, was also present in crowd. He was moved by the spectacle and delighted to find that Bruce had attended the same college.

Bruce was soon teaching Kung Fu around the neighborhood. His students included judo student DeMile, Jesse Glover and many others. The classes were held in a backyard, or in a garage. After finishing his job at Ruby Chow, Bruce began classes in Ruby Chow's garage.

DeMile was friends to a Japanese-American named Takauki Kmura, who owned a town supermarket. Takauki immigrated from Japan during the Second World War. He was a Judo student. DeMile encouraged him to attend Bruce classes because he thought he'd be interested to learn more about the new Karate Kid. Kimura initially refused to use the suggestion, but DeMile convinced him to give it a try. Bruce's style and techniques captivated Kimura during his visit. Bruce's fast moves were only part of what he was drawn to. What impressed him most was his ability infuse Confucius and Taoist philosophy during training sessions. He could not resist joining the classes.

Takuki wasn't able to find any common ground with him beyond the classes at the beginning. Bruce kept pushing Takuki towards spending more time with him. They were from the same continent. After days of awkward attempts at starting a conversation Bruce struck a chord with Takuki. The two started talking on a daily base after the classes. His conversations proved to be invaluable for Takuki, who was struggling with midlife crises. Bruce made Takuki see the value of his humanity and that of a Japanese immigrant.

Bruce fell in love with Amy Sanbo-a Japenese migrant. They talked long hours about their lives, their future plans, as well as their goals for their lives. He was a man she respected for his dedication and determinism in his art. But, it took her a while to realize his incomprehensible view of life. She used to listen to him raving about his Kung Fu classes and his goals for life. She was never able to hear him, even though he was always attentive. When she accused him sometimes of being showy, he would often quote Taoisms and Confucianism. She wanted to be writer but he saw her choice as futile and suggested that she help him.

Many of his closest acquaintances called him a true chauvinist. Sometimes, he was unable to even show any compassion for others. He often stated that he could make his own way out from poverty. Why shouldn't others? His incompassionate attitude was carried with him to his classes. He did not show his moves more than two times, and never asked his students if their understanding was good. As in every classroom, there was always one student who couldn't understand his master's instructions. His close friend Takuki was this student. Bruce never gave in to their repeated pleas for an explanation. Kimura gave up after many unsuccessful attempts. Bruce told him that he had potential but he didn't recognize it. This gave him a new boost of energy. He decided to try again. Bruce taught him how to be his assistant, making training even more difficult.

After working with his students for a long time, Brue began giving demonstrations to local television stations. He had every intention of everything going according to plan during his demonstrations. However, much to his dismay, the events did not turn out as planned. His students were always guilty of some kind of mishap, and they had to deal with the consequences after the demonstrations.

He would tell his students a story about an old lady, to help them feel better. In the story, an elderly lady's house sets on fire one day. She considered the piano to be her most valuable possession. When the house was on fire, she took the piano to a safe spot. It took approximately four young and healthy men to move the piano to its rightful place after the fire was out. The story also clarified his source of energy, which wasn't in muscles, but was within his heart. His inner strength enabled him to defeat the tallest, strongest and fastest of his opponents with just one hit.

Bruce still played pranks with his friends in adulthood just as he did during his childhood. He bought different colors of lenses. He preferred the pair with blood vessels as the lenses. He used those lenses to order Chinese at a Chinese restaurant. One of his friends pretended that he was speaking Chinese. This trick was used many times and scared off many waiters.

He inhibited multiple shades inside him. He could be playing pranks or lecturing about Confucianism and Taoism at one time. He would change his personality according to the situation or person. His ability to switch between personality types was often cited as one of his greatest assets.

Bruce was a staunch opponent to harassment of the weaker and the stronger. He never allowed injustices to happen before his eyes. When he was walking with his friends down Chinatown's main street, he saw a girl being harassed and pushed by a few men in a vehicle. Bruce approached them and demanded that they stop harassing her. Bruce knocked one of them on the face for not acting smartly when one of them tried to act smart.

He did not realize the darker side of his inner strength which could take him to greater heights. He never attempted to master it, understand it, or even see it.

The Inner Conflicts

Bruce had many fights in his life, but his biggest was with himself. As I mentioned, Bruce has been sleeping since childhood. Many nights, he would kick and talk to himself in his dreams. He had an incredible amount of energy in his body, which was sometimes his biggest blessing, but at other times it was his biggest problem.

One of the most misunderstood or misrepresented events in his history is his fight with a force within his dreams several minutes after he arrived at Chow's. Many people associate him with craft, demonic abilities, hallucination and others. It was a terrible event. None of the above explanations are able to explain the enormity of what happened in his life. Bruce Lee transformed the world after this episode. The episode could be explained by him facing his dark side. He was trying to overcome his chauvinisms and anger, as well as his impulsiveness.

A few months after the incident, he completed his schooling with enough grades to qualify for a seat on the Washington University's Seattle campus.

He began college in March 1961. He was a fan of gymnastics, English, and wrestling. With an eye on his future, he enrolled in theatre speech and speech improvement classes. He took classes in Chinese philosophy and composition, Chinese psychology, psychology and adjustment, leadership and Chinese language. He felt a rush in his ambitions, accompanied with a rush to reach his new goals. He was driven by his ambitions to live in the land where dreams were realized, but he felt homesick and decided to write about his experience in Hong Kong.

As the days passed, attendance at his classes increased. He had other plans. He was less interested in teaching and more focused on learning during his classes. He experimented and tried new moves with his pupils. Because he was staging larger demonstrations, it was impossible for him to lose to anyone. He was about for a great adventure. He was going to encounter fighters that were larger and more powerful than him. His technique was what would help him keep at the top. He was forced to practice his moves.

His fear of being defeated never materialized and there were many factors which made him invincible and the best throughout his life. His ability to dissect the most difficult moves and philosophies into simpler, more manageable forms is the first. He was also able to retain and process large amounts information in a very short time. Last but not least, his high level and constant motivation. It was this passion that kept him interested in learning new styles. This motivated him to travel through California and Canada meeting Kung Fu masters and learning their styles. His encounters with different styles and masters led him to realize the ineffectiveness that was being taught across the continent. It was the inability of their saviors, to help them develop them over time that was a problem that he found common with all styles. He found most of them too slow to use in real-life. Thus, he lost a lot of respect for traditional styles and Kung Fu methods.

He was vocal about his dislike of the old techniques of fighting and his belief they are too inefficient for everyday life. Uechi, who was studying Japanese black belt Karate, heckled Bruce at one point. He was speaking out about his frustration with inapt techniques during one his demonstrations. Uechi was persistent in his heckling despite Bruce's assurance that his criticisms were not meant to be personal. Bruce was tired and gave up. He asked the Japanese to come to his hand to face him later. The venue and date were agreed upon. The pair met at the local YMCA handball court, accompanied only by a small group of spectators. The referee gave green for the fight to start. Bruce aligned himself in the Wing Chun stance while Bruce put his feet on the ground. Bruce won the fight in less then ten seconds. He was rendered unable to move by his opponent after the first hit on his stomach.

Few of his pupils were able to learn from him the skill and patience that was required for his teachings to be successful. He was not like other kung Fu teachers and did not give a simple way to do Kung Fu. His methods required extreme dedication, hard work, and a commitment that not many could make.

Allen Joe, a famed martial artist of his era, became interested in Bruce Lee's potential future. He followed him to Ruby Chow's restaurant. He waited patiently and ordered dishes after dishes, while enjoying his scotch. Finally, when they did finally meet, he showed Bruce some of their moves. Bruce smiled and showed him techniques to block his moves. Allen Joe was impressed with his dexterity and asked him for his Kung Fu methods. Bruce showed him the Hong Kong wood dummy that he had brought from Hong Kong. This was the dummy on which he practiced the moves. It was named after Bodhidharma, the Buddhist monk.

Bruce was not only known for his fighting skills but also because of his charisma through his words. Bruce, twenty years old, was invited to Garfield High School to lecture on Chinese Philosophy. He arrived with Amy Sanbo, his then girlfriend. Linda Emery (17) was one such head.

Amy and he have been dating for three year. He tried to propose marriage many times but was denied. In 1963, he wanted to tell his family about his relationship with Amy. Amy was offered an internship in New York the following year. Amy was still debating whether to accept. Bruce wanted Amy not to accept the offer and to marry him. He proposed to her once more and offered his grandmother's wedding ring.

Amy refused his second proposal.

Hong Kong: Vacationing

Bruce went to Hong Kong with his devastated family in 1963. Doug Palmer, his student, and his friend had been taking Mandarin classes at the University. Bruce was not tempted to refuse the offer to go with him to Hong Kong.

But he didn't realize it was Cantonese they spoke in Hong Kong and not Mandarin. Mandarin and Cantonese are the two main dialects of China. This is why it's fascinating for a linguist to study this topic. Mandarin is China's national language. It is also one among the few official languages in the UN. It is also one of five languages that are spoken in central China. It is sometimes mistakenly referred to as an offshoot language of Mandarin. But the obvious differences between Mandarin (and Cantonese) confirms that Cantonese truly is a separate language. Mandarin and Cantonese share the same tonal languages. This means that one term can have several connotations depending on the context and the pronunciation. Mandarin has seven tones while Cantonese only 9 tones. Mandarin however, has seven tones. Despite the fact that these languages use similar typescripts, the pronunciation of the words can be so different that some people like to call it chicken talking with ducks.

Bruce and Doug were never bored at Honk Kong. They tried many different activities that summer. They took a stroll along the busy streets of Hong Kong. Bruce was a funny man, and he often played practical jokes in public places. They worked often together and were fond of the police officers as their target.

Bruce loved dressing up geekily when he wasn't practicing. People would often call him a nerd. His fashion sense made him a popular target of street gangsters. Bruce and Doug were returning in a ferry from one of the islands when two hoodlums began to make fun of him. He ignored them for a while and, after a few minutes, he kicked one of the hoodlums with a punch. The other was perplexed.

Bruce wanted to spend some time in Hong Kong with Yip Man, his former trainer. He advised Doug to keep his secrets from YipMan, since it could damage his traditionalist beliefs. YipMan is required to teach only Chinese martial arts. Bruce and Yip Man started spending long hours practicing at the top of their apartments. The practice sessions would go on for many hours, beginning in the morning and continuing until the evening.

Bruce found his childhood crush Pak Yan in Hong Kong. This star was in the Cantonese film business. The two of them used to meet up on a regular basis. Pak Yan received several roles in movies during his time in Pakistan.

Before he went to Seattle, his father demanded that he be circumcised. Amazingly, he agreed. The operation was extremely painful and he preferred to wear loose clothes for the following weeks. "Had i known that it would so painful, i would not have agreed to it. " He stopped practicing Kung Fu until all the pain was gone.

Bruce and Doug stopped at Hawaii while they were on their way towards Seattle. A local school asked them to present a demonstration in Hawaii. The demonstration was well attended by many people. A man was sitting in a corner with his cigarette smoking and was keenly watching the demonstration. Bruce approached him, and he began to ask questions. Bruce blocked his move, and he was then asked to follow suit. Bruce left him and immediately snapped towards Bruce saying, 'you left an empty space.' Bruce, however, was amused and didn't react. Bruce blocked the man's attempt to show Bruce a different move later. Bruce then held him between both his fists, causing him to light his cigarettes.

After returning to the United States, his realization was that the country's government had different plans. He was invited to join the Vietnam war. He was sent for a physical exam and, thankfully he was found unfit.

Linda Emery was the first to graduate from that school, where Bruce had been a guest lecturer. Bruce began her college studies with her. Bruce was then studying philosophy. Sue Ann Kay, her Chinese friend, was accompanying Bruce to one of the practice session in Seattle's Chinatown. The sessions were held inside a rusty basement.

Students began to discuss Bruce's Kung Fu classes soon. Linda Emery joined the University also as a student. After a long day at the university, his classes became increasingly popular and everyone was looking forward to them. Bruce then applied to the University for permission to hold a demonstration in University's men's gymnasium. It was a huge success. The number of participants in these classes rose to an all-time high.

Linda was invited to a dinner by him one day after the class.

Going to Chapel

Bruce Lee was now a girlfriend of Linda Emery. Bruce loved to talk, and Linda was a good listener made them a great match. He was still at Chow's and was looking to find a place where he could move out and start new classes. Linda was the inspiration behind his actions. Linda was the inspiration for Bruce moving out to start classes at a rented location.

Bruce decided to rent a space on the ground level of an apartment block located at 4750 University Way after looking through advertisements in newspapers. He fixed the cost of the classes at $4 per week. He could afford his living expenses and rent easily. Bruce gave Chows the notice in October 1963. He opened his new institute named Jun Fan Gung Fu Institute.

The new space was pre-installed with showers but no windows. Bruce and some of his students furnished the new space with items that he brought back from Hong Kong. These things gave the place an authentic Chinese touch.

Bruce and Linda began spending more quality time together once classes had begun at the new school. Linda kept the secret relationship from her parents. Although her parents were Protestants and wanted their daughter to marry in the same faith as them, she knew that they would have to deal with the consequences. Linda asked Bruce many times their future when they were dating in secret. He just smiled when they replied.

He gave a demonstration at Garfield High School with Doug Palmer in December 1963. This was also the same school that Doug had attended a year earlier than

Linda. Bruce was about show the students the move that was to be his trademark over the next few years. He wanted to show them the "one inch punch."

He began his demonstration by giving a traditional talk about Kung Fu's history. He then explained to his students, most of whom were beginning Karate, the difference in a Kung Fu kick from a Karate Kick. The students were not interested in his talk, and seemed to be bored to death. He then asked one student to volunteer. A tall, powerful boy offered his help. Many students were still asleep when he raised his hand. He told them he was going for one inch of distance and that he would punch him. Doug asked Doug to take the chair from behind the man. He then lean forward and reached for the guy with both hands, his fist tightened. He punched him in the chest in a flash and then he flew forwards landing on the chair.

Bruce kept in touch at all times with an Oakland Kung Fu teacher. James Lee was his full name. Bruce and James set out to open the Oakland's second branch of the Jun Fan Gung Fu Institute. Bruce had lost touch with his studies by this point and had given up his plans to finish the University of Washington's Philosophy doctorate. James accepted his proposal and began planning for the move from Washington to Oakland. He sold the car and had all his furniture shipped to Oakland. Before he left for Oakland, he promised Linda he would marry Linda when he is able to support a family.

Oakland is the county seat in Alameda County (California), United States. It is the third biggest city in San Francisco Bay Area. Also, it is the eighth largest city of California, the 45th largest in America. It is a major West Coast city port and the largest city of the East Bay region in the

San Francisco Bay Area. It is home to 419,267 people according to 2015 data. It acts as a centre for trade in San Francisco Bay Area. In fact, the Port of Oakland has the highest traffic in Northern California, San Francisco Bay and is the fifth busiest in America. It is located six miles (9.7km east) of San Francisco. Oakland was established by the United States government in 1852.

Long Beach Convention and Entertainment Center is located in Long Beach. It hosted the Karate Tournament every July 1964. The crowd was cheering on the players as Bruce Lee, an Asian gentleman, made an announcement that he would be demonstrating a traditional martial art called Kung Fu. Bruce entered the arena, wearing a simple, black Kung Fu costume and slippers. Bruce started the demonstration with a one finger push up, and then ended it with a "one inch punch" on one contestant. His intention was to show the public that Kung Fu had more energy-efficient punching techniques than he did.

Dan Inosanto, a Filipino fighter, was on the other side of Dan Inosanto's punch. According to Dan Inosanto, the incident left him stunned. He resolved to train alongside Bruce and tracked him down back to his hotel room.

Bruce and Dan became fast friends and began to meet at trainings. Dan arranged that Bruce would give demonstrations throughout San Francisco. The San Francisco demonstrations were very similar to his other shows. There were fast kicks and punches, as well as blocks. Don also learned a lot from him while spending time with them.

Bruce and Linda maintained constant communication via letters. Bruce proposed marriage soon after, and Linda accepted his proposal. They decided to get married secretly in Oakland, before contacting their parents. Bruce returned home with a wedding ring in hand on the 12th, August 1964. Linda's parents tried to hide the marriage, but Linda's aunt saw the details of the marriage in the local newspaper. As every aunt, she phoned Linda's mother to complain about not having received an invitation. Linda's mother was shocked and confused when her son called.

The Emerys tried all possible tactics to persuade the couple that they should end the marriage. However, Linda's pregnancy with his child led to the Emerys making arrangements for the marriage. Seattle Congregational Church was chosen for the wedding venue. Bruce wore the suit he rented at a local boutique, and Linda lacked a wedding dress. Taky was the best man, as well as the only one to be invited from outside of the family.

Fight Train Fight

Bruce and James Lee were partners in the founding of the second branch at his Kung Fu school, which was located in Oakland. Bruce and Linda married when Bruce was still living in Oakland. James Lee, his wife, and Bruce were happy to host them until Bruce found accommodation. James Lee's spouse died of cancer within months of the couple moving in. She had a young son, and daughter. Linda took over the care of her children. James Lee asked Bruce to move in with them, rather than finding another housing for Linda and him.

Bruce was twenty years younger to James Lee. He had been a stateweight lifting champion, an amateur boxer, and a brownbelt in Judo. He had to work as welder in order to make his living. James had trained in traditional Kung Fu. But he was unhappy with the way it was taught and the method of training. He later developed his own informal style, which incorporated moves from Kung Fu as well as other martial arts. Bruce and James both shared the same vision of making Kung Fu more adaptable to real combat situations.

They opened the second Jun Fan Gung Fu center at Broadway Street in Oakland. It was initially a failure, with less footfall. But, fortunately, the profit from the branch at Seattle helped to keep it afloat. Bruce never made exaggerated claims in his advertisements for Kung Fu classes. He didn't claim to be able teach the art in 6 months or 1 year like other Kung Fu schools. He didn't want to see students in a hurry to learn the art. Instead, he wanted dedicated pupils who would persevere in learning the art. He did not want his students to be able to learn the art without being inspired. His classes started to get better attendance and he was challenged to a fight by Wong Jak Man (a new Kung Fu instructor) in the area.

Bruce arrived in the country with a lot of Kung Fu knowledge, but most of it was passed on to the Chinese community. The outsiders could not learn anything. Bruce came along with the same goal of creating equality for all people regardless their race. He chose to accept anyone, no matter what race or color they were, into his school as long as their hearts were positive and happy. Taky Kimura recalled that he took them in. However, when he left San Francisco where the Chinese community was more like China, they took exception and forced him to fight his own way out.

Jak Man was a recent arrival from Hong Kong, with the intention of teaching Kung Fu in America. He was 5'10" tall and weighed 135lbs. Although he was an expert in Shaolin, he also trained in internal Kung Fu techniques. Bruce Lee was the best Kung Fu instructor in the area, so he decided to take on the challenge to make his mark in the Kung Fu world. He challenged him to a match. The winner would become the school's director, and the loser would cease teaching martial arts.

The fight's date and location were set. The ground rules include no eye jabs, no kicks to the groin, and so forth. They were created before the fight. Bruce Lee made an inquisitive comment about Wong Jack Man, a friend who had helped to set the fight up. He said, "You've just been killed by your friend."

Wong Jack Man moved forward with a quick lance handshake and cleared the floor. Bruce moved forward quickly and extended his lance hand to his eyes. Wong was amazed, but quickly developed into the traditional Kung Fu form of fighting. Bruce, on the other hand, adopted a Wing chun pose. Although both men were in static positions, Bruce was much more aggressive. Wong and Bruce continued fighting for long periods. Bruce could not finish the fight. Linda Lee claimed Wong was running for safety and cover. But Wong's supporters disagree. They tried unsuccessfully to disarm Bruce, but Jim Lee intervened. The fight was called off after a while.

He was challenged by the San Francisco Chinese martial arts community in Oakland. His challenge required that Bruce stop teaching non-Chinese students and Caucasian students, if he wins. Bruce had a very formal challenge when the Chinese martial arts artist came to Oakland from San Francisco. It was my eighth month of pregnancy with Brandon, James lee, and I was there. This fight with the Chinese fighter lasted three minutes. It was a marathon. Bruce pursued the Chinese martial art as he ran across the room. Bruce finally managed to grab him and take him to the ground. The Chinese martial arts artist was defeated. They all fled. Linda Lee spoke out to say that Bruce won the right of teaching anyone he wanted'.

Bruce was a highly self-critical person and felt dissatisfied by his performance in the fight. He felt deeply hurt by the fact it took him longer than three minutes for him to finish the fight. He started thinking about ways to improve both his punches, and kicks. His punches, kicks, and power were the most important thing to him. Although he was able to master the technique, his ch'i wasn't quite up to scratch.

James Lee provided support and he started an intensive training course in physical therapy. He started each day by meditating for hours. Then, he would run for several miles. During his run, he was accompanied by two of his dogs. After finishing his lunch, the dog accompanied him on the run. He then spent hours training on his bike. Long sessions of sit ups were the highlight of his evenings. He sometimes lifted weights to strengthen his forearms. He was able to gain more muscle than ever before in no time. He included protein drinks and weight-gain drinks to meet his protein requirements. He also took high doses of vitamins into his diet.

James Lee, his friend & trainer, says that he "trained insane". He would train until he lost his breath. When he got it back, he'd start over again. He never stopped learning.

Even though he was out, he didn't miss any chance to practice his moves. He used to practice kicks on trees. To master his kicks, the litter was blown by garbage. Those were the days before machines could be used to practice martial arts. Bruce and James Lee felt the immediate need and began designing and building many machines that would allow him to train in martial arts.

James Lee soon found his garage stuffed with all types of machines like heavy bags for punching or air filled kicking shields. There was also a loop and pulley device that could stretch the legs. Bruce's Hong Kong-imported Wing Chun wooden doll was modified according to his training.

During training sessions at his institute he tried every trick to get the students' real emotions of fear and anger up to fight. After months of hard training and dedication his punches were at their best and could fly an ordinary person into the air. He decided to test his moves only on a wooden dummy because they were too dangerous to be applied to a human. Many who had been holding the kicking box for him ended in dislocating their shoulder blades.

Before the Big Break

"Water is the simplest substance in the entire world. Yet, it can penetrate most rocks and other hard materials. You can name it. It is insubstantial. That means you cannot grasp it, punch it, or hit it with your fists to inflict damage. This is what every Kung Fu fighter aspires for. To be soft as water and flexible to adapt to its opponent.

Here is an excerpt taken from Bruce Lee's first screen-test for a part on a TV show about a Chinese Detective. How did he manage to land a screen-test? He was lucky enough to get the screen test. Bruce performed a Kung Fu demonstration in Long Beach, California on August 2, 1964. His 'one-inch punch' and his two finger push-ups inspired the crowd. Jay Sebring, who was the hair stylist on the Batman TV series, was also present. He was reminded of Bruce's genius long before William dozier became a T.V. A producer was looking to cast an actor in a TV series about Chinese detectives. Sebring then presented a Long Beach film of Bruce's demonstration. Dozier was impressed, and requested that Bruce fly down to Los Angeles to test the screen.

A 24-year-old Bruce Lee auditions for a TV series in Los Angeles on February 1, 1965. He was only nineteen months away from his first T.V. appearance. Kato, The Green Hornet

"And you went for college in the United States?"

Bruce replied "Yes"

"And what've you done?"

'Em.Philosophy'

Bruce initially displayed signs of nervousness while wearing a dark suit, a white shirt, a small tie and a knot. He would only pick up the form. As more questions were placed in his field of expertise, he felt more confident each time.

"And you worked at motion pictures in Hong Kong?" asked the interviewer.

"Yes, I was six years ago."

"You said earlier that jujitsu is not the strongest or most effective form of oriental fighting. What is the best and most powerful form of oriental fighting?

Bruce replied, "Well it is bad to say so the best, but I think Kung Fu looks pretty good."

"Well, tell me a bit about Kung Fu.

It originated in China and is the ancestor to Jujitsu (Karate) and Jujitsu. It's more complete and fluid.

What is the difference between Kung Fu punches and Karate punches?

He said that the karate punch was like being hit with an Iron Bar-WHACK!

America's most recent experiences with martial arts, up to 1965, were Judo/Jujitsu. They were introduced through Japanese arts which were taught to soldiers during Korea War. Bruce considered himself to be an ambassador for Chinese martial arts.

He was an expert in Kung Fu but his interest in philosophy made him wonder why martial artists (Chinese or not) were so hesitant to preserve tradition. Or to look deeper into the matter to discover the truth. He devised his own Kung Fu technique, which he described to be non-classical. It was based on the principles economic of motion, simplicity, directness, and simplicity.

Bruce explained, "For instance you will read it from a magazine and you will learn that when someone grabs you, they will first do this then this then this then this then and so on and so forth." Kung Fu involves fast movements. It is not the ideal idea to do too many stepping, stepping, and then let go. This is what simplicity means. It's the same in striking as it is in everything. It must be based upon a minimum of motion so that every movement is directly expression of one motion.

The interviewer was moved by his belief of Kung Fu and asked him to show some of the moves.

Interviewer asked: "Show us some moves?"

Bruce replied, "Well, I know it's difficult to do it alone, but we will try our best."

Bruce is assisted by a volunteer, who then walks in to assist him.

Bruce stated, "I will go ahead even though all accidents do happen," before he showed his moves.

While taking a Kung Fu stand, he said that there were many kinds of strikes.

He continued: "To your eyes you would use your fingers." He asked the volunteer to relax and assured him he wouldn't be hurt.

He exclaimed, "Straight to the face from waist, and everything else," while directing the fist towards the volunteer's face.

"Let us move the other direction." This will make it easier for you to do it in front of the camera," interrupted the interviewer.

Bruce said that pen arm strike is when the waist is again inserted into the back fist. Chinese are known for their ability to hit low from high, right down to the groin.

His moves were all new to the audience. These moves were performed at a much slower speed than his usual so many times they were unnoticed.

Jeet Kune Do

Bruce had three Kung Fu schools open in America by February 1967. The schools were in Los Angeles, Oakland and Seattle.

Based on his investigation into the unarmed combat, he taught his own explanations of the martial art at his schools. Bruce was critical of the limitations and traditions in the martial art by this time. They were taught in schools across the globe. However, they lack a solid grounding of reality. The self-defense techniques were mostly rehearsed, and most of them were used in a predetermined pattern. Because he had experienced real combat, he realized that it is spontaneous and not planned. He discovered that these were chaotic and irregular rhythms that martial artists cannot anticipate, but that martial artists can only respond. The karate tournaments of his time were non-contact and decided mainly on points. A team made up of judges determined who was the victor. The judges determined which combatant would most likely have caused injury to the other combatant if contact was allowed. Bruce found such styles ineffective. He called such pseudo fighting organized despair and dryland pooling. It is possible to trace his criticism of the art to his Hong Kong history, where he participated in not so structured karate tournaments as well as street fights and challenge match. These fights and matches took place on Hong Kong's rooftops. He had also fought regularly against opponents who were armed with knives, chains, or other lethal weaponry. Referees were rarely needed in such encounters. Instead of being involved in traditional karate competitions, he decided to focus his efforts on creating a scientific approach to weaponsless fighting. His research led to Newtonian physics and the methods of western boxing and European fencing. These are proficiency driven techniques, not like the Chinese martial art. It was through this research that he learned that the only test for a combative technique's worthiness is its ability to be landed on an adversary. He removed all patterns from his style, and retained only the techniques that he has decided to use in a true self-defense situation. He was most likely the first martial artist to require his students to wear headgear, boxing gloves and body protectors. This practice helped to create the modern style of fighting known as Mix Martial Arts. Nothing was planned. At his classes, there was no fighting and only full contact reality-based martial arts were the norm. In 1967, he introduced the notion of a full-contactscuffling at the International karate tournament in long beach California. He did not stress defensive moves in his reality-based approach. However, it would have allowed an enemy to set the tone and pace of the fight. In his new style, he focused more on attack. Or rather, intercepting the opponent's attack with a one-of-a kind attack. In the middle of 1967, he realized that the most fundamental characteristic of his new style was the principle and practice of intervention. He decided to call his new method Jeet Kune Do.

Bruce wrote in his book 'Tao of Jeet Kune Do" that security means turning the unlimited living into something dead and a chosen pattern of limits. Jeet Kune Do can be understood by letting go of all ideas, patterns, and styles. Can you view a situation with no name? Naming it is like giving it a name.

Jeet Kune Do is also known as JKD. It is the most modern Gung Fu system. Jeet Kung Do is Bruce Lee's original idea to combine Wing Chun Kung Fu, American Boxing, French Fencing and Grappling into one ultimate combat art. Bruce Lee passed away in the style was it was being created. This is a different style than other traditional martial art because Bruce used his individual experience and understanding to create what many now consider the most popular self-defense technique. Mixed Martial Arts, also called Jeet Kune Do, is a term that has been used many times.

Bruce believed that simplicity was the key to effective self-defense. Research into different forms of martial arts revealed that they had many reactions to one form of attack. He found that certain martial arts could deal with more than one type of punch. This made it difficult to see how they would do in a real fight. He set about creating a style with a simple, direct solution. This is what led to his love for concurrent block-and-hit because it made countering an attack easier. He was taught this technique in Wing Chun. Later, he integrated it with the idea'stop-hitting' which is a counteroffensive technique in Western fencing. This technique required the practitioner to lead using his/her principal handed. Bruce realized that Western fencing was possible without the sword when he stood in an attacking position. He also applied the concept of stop-hitting to the empty-hand system. Bruce believed that the best way for an opponent to attack him is to intercept his attack with a stop-hit from his strong leg or hand. So, he created Jeet Kune Don, his martial art that focuses on intercepting fists.

Green Hornet

After his first screen test, he lost his father's funeral a week later. Linda stayed home and he had no choice but to fly to Hong Kong. He stopped using his legs when he reached his father's grave. To be able to climb up to his father's coffin, he needed to work hard. His father had a tradition that required him to confess his sins and be at his side when he died. You can speculate that his deep sobbing may have satisfied the tradition's requirements.

Bruce returned to Oakland two more weeks later. The next day, Bruce returned to Oakland. He received a call from William Dozier letting him know that the series for which his audition was unsuccessful had been cancelled. But, because of his audition, he was chosen for another part in a series called Green Hornet.

Bruce and Linda, with their unborn baby, boarded a flight to Hong Kong in May 1965. He needed to settle a dispute over his father's property in Hong Kong. Linda's trip to China proved more challenging than she imagined. First, the humidity was a nuisance for the child but eventually for Linda. Sometimes, the child would cry for hours, making it difficult for her mother to sleep at night. She also struggled with language barriers between her and her mother. Added to it, she had very different food preferences. She wasn't prepared to experience the culture shock in Hong Kong.

Bruce maintained constant contact with Green Hornet's producers in the States during their stay. He was always on the phone, asking when the shooting would start. He had even planned on visiting Yip Man while in Hong Kong. He had a favor to request.

He wanted Yip Man to do Kung Fu stunts to show his students back home in America. Yip Man refused, as he did with all conservative Gurus. He returned home disappointed, feeling self-reproach for not asking him for it in the first instance. He returned to Seattle, where he stayed for a while with Linda's family. He sat there waiting for the producers call. As he waited to hear from producers, he spent his time reading the philosophical works of various new and old world sages as well the spiritual gurus in the Oriental world. Buddha, Lao Tzu and Krishnamurti were his favourite philosophers. The long reading sessions took their toll on his back, and he started suffering from backache.

The wait was finally over. William Dozier called him, informing him that the shooting would start in three month's time. He and Linda moved in to an apartment in Los Angeles, March 1966. He was about to get $400 for each Green Hornet Episode.

Green Hornet began in radio as a program in the late 1930s. It was continued in the 50's. It is a fictional character. An incognito crime-fighter. The idea was developed by George W. Trendle (with input from James Jewell), and Fran Striker. It was first broadcast on WXYZ Detroit, Mutual Network and NBC Blue, in 1936. Fran Striker, George W. Trendle, and Fran

Striker also worked on Lone Ranger's radio series in the past. Al Hodge was Donovan Faust (Robert Hall), Jack McCarthy and Jack McCarthy called the radio series Green Hornet. The theme song of the radio program was "Flight of the Bumblebee." Other noises were added in the background.

Green Hornet and Kato combine martial arts with other weapons such as gas guns to tackle crime in the capital. They drive around the city in their car they call "the Black Beauty", but Kato was originally described as a Japanese martial art artist. After the attack on Pearl Harbor, Kato became a Filipino. Kato's role on radio was initially performed by Raymond Hayashi, Roland Parker, and then later by Mickey Tolan. Bruce Lee portrayed him in the 1966 television series.

Bruce's portrayal Kato made the series a hit in the United States as well as Hong

Kong. Van Williams played the role of Green Hornet. After the completion of one season with twenty-six episodes it contained, the series was canceled. While the televised series was based upon the radio show of the 1930s, the format was not the same. Bruce's Kato character used green sleeve daggers in television series as an alternative attack when hand-to-hand combat was too risky. The episode in which Robin was seen fighting Kato was the most popular. The end result was tied. The series has been adapted into many comic books and movies over the years. It also made Green Hornet a popular character in mainstream comics.

Green Hornet was more for Bruce than just his first appearance on the TV screen. It gave him an opportunity to showcase his talent to the world. For the first times in his life, he could show what he'd been practicing for nearly his entire life to such a large audience. Kung Fu and Bruce Lee were household names in America and Hong Kong. Unknowingly, they would be synonymous with each other in the years to come, breaking down all barriers and reaching new heights within the company of one another.

The Tryst with Hollywood

Bruce opened his third Kung Fu Training School at 628 College Street. This was in Los Angeles' Chinatown area. It was just a few streets from the Dodger Stadium. He preferred privacy at school. Therefore, he painted the windows black to hide it from prying eyes. He now taught more students than 50 under one roof, and it was only getting bigger every day. He found it increasingly difficult to keep up with all the students. Dan Inosanto was a good assistant. He made it a restriction on the number of students who were already trained as martial artists and who showed talent.

Bruce displayed different sides to his personality throughout the training. Sometimes he was calm and relaxed, while other times he was tensed, strict, and anxious. He was flexible and could change his mood according to the circumstances. One time, the interactions between him & his students became too informal and casual for him. He decided to take the necessary steps. He asked his students to stop calling him by his name, and instead call him 'sifu' (the Chinese word for master).

He did not find such an exercise futile or unnecessary unlike his days with Yip man, when his patience, dedication, and perseverance were tested. It seemed far removed from reality. He was always looking for a way to separate himself from the Kung Fu traditional teaching styles.

He always placed a high emphasis on personal health and developed a personalized fitness program to meet the needs of each student. He was an excellent teacher, but his biggest problem was his temperament. He often got into arguments with his students, almost always causing serious injuries. Dan Inosanto, his friend, was also his assistant.

He was not quick to lose his temper. It used to disappear as soon as it appeared. Sometimes he displayed the other side of him and was very compassionate. Dan received an expensive set if weights from him that he had been wanting for a long time but could not afford.

The past is repeating itself. Bruce was again challenged for a fight by two local mafia artists, just like in Oakland. After his previous experiences with such confrontations, he didn't succumb the temptation to beat those two martial arts but wisely turned them down.

In an effort to increase his income, he began giving private tuitions starting at 50$/hour. He now gave private tuitions at 50$ an hour to Hollywood stars. Jimmy Coburn, Steve McQueen, and many other stars were among his list of students. Bruce Lee's guidance was an inspiration to many in the Karate community.

Bruce's encounter with Karate is part of a long history. Karate was popularized by American soldiers who had served in Japan and Korea during World War II and Korea War III respectively. Ed Parker organized The Long Beach Tournament in 1960, which saw Bruce give a stunning demonstration of Kung Fu. The Karate scene was rapidly changing. Chuck Norris, who is the American Karate Community's most famous figure, successfully combined Japanese and Korean martial arts. He incorporated Korean kicking styles and Korean punching techniques into his style. Bruce had to adapt quickly.

Bruce was a voracious reader when he wasn't training. His library had a large selection of books. Most of his books were about one or the other type of fighting. His collection contained everything, including boxing guides and Karate magazines. It didn't matter if the book was about fighting, it would end up in his library. He loved those books and considered them the treasure troves for knowledge. He also owned books on archery and dancing. His library collection showed his interest in philosophy. He also read the works of Confucius as well as Lao Tzu and other Chinese philosophers. He also had books by Khalil Gabran and Krishnamurti in his library. He even had a collection that included videos of some of history's most famous fights. His favorite boxing match was between Sandy Saddler (Willie Pep) on September 26, 1951. He was a huge fan of Muhammad Ali. He often practiced his punches looking in the mirror.

It was one to know him only as a teacher. But it was quite another thing to call him a friend. Both roles were different, but he had a charm about him that many considered magic. His Karate instructors were among the top names in American Karate. Before they were able to learn from him, they all had been great fighters. His Karate students had great respect for him, but he was hated and ignorant in Kung Fu. He was seen by the traditional martial art community as an outsider whose means were limited to street fighting. He didn't notice that their views were influential. During his training, however, he continued to flout the traditional Kung Fu rules.

He encouraged his trainees to practice their skills as closely as possible in real combat situations. He taught only the essential skills necessary to win a fight. He only used the punches & kicks he thought were sufficient to win the fight. Many Kung Fu masters dismissed the techniques as juvenile. His Kung Fu principles of 'adapt and innovate' were less accepted.

His first attempt at boxing won him the interschool championship. Later, he fenced with his brother, a Commonwealth Games Champion. We also know from earlier chapters that he practiced t'aichi with his father in his youth. His specialization was Wing Chun. He had been practicing it all his adult life. Before he arrived in America, he learned other martial arts like 'praying mantis", 'eagle claw' and 'hung gar'. In America, Taky Kimura was the one who introduced him Judo. He then continued to improve his

Judo skills by studying with Jesse Glover (Sato) and Jesse Glover (Jesse). While practicing with Dan Inosanto he tried his hand at Filipino martial art. Gene La Belle was Gene's friend on the set of Green Hornet. They shared moves that were similar to each other. Wally Jay was another jujitsu expert who he had many good encounters with and training sessions. He trained in Thai boxing, westernboxing, and French footfighting. He had been exposed to nearly all forms of combat, which allowed him to cherry pick the best moves while developing his own style.

Even though he was busy training, meditation was an integral part of his daily life. He meditated every single day, as he searched for ways to increase his ch'i.

Bruce, unlike other Kung Fu teachers who could take classes of hundreds of students at once, was able to keep his class small with his professionalism and unique teaching methods. Therefore, he couldn't open more schools. For his own financial security, he was forced to teach private lessons.

While teaching in Hollywood he had the idea to act in Kung Fu movies. It was actually always there in his thoughts. He had even made plans to film a Shaolin warrior priest. This priest used his Kung Fu skills in fighting crime in the city. He took his idea to Tom Kuhn (TV producer), who suggested the name "Warrior".

Famous screenwriter Stirling Silliphant and James Coburn were among his celebrity pupils. Silliphant heard about Vic Damone's battle with his bodyguards. It was a story that was being circulated in Hollywood's social networks.

Vic Damone, a popular singer in the 50s and 60s, was there to witness his strength-

and strategic genius - personally in 1968. Damone, in his prime in the late 1960s, assumed that he had the best two man security workforce money could purchase. Bruce was adamant about trying to outdo them. Damone was instructed to give Bruce the impression of putting him 'on his ans and teaching him a lessons'. Bruce suggested that Bruce could offer Damone a lesson. Bruce said that he wanted Damone to see how he could easily bypass his first bodyguard. The second would then light a cigarette.

Bruce explained that the cigarette signifies a gun and that his bodyguard had have to remove it from Bruce's mouth before Bruce can kick it. Bruce claims that Bruce was going to perform all of the moves, including the entry, the kicking of a cigarette kick, and reaching Damone through his bodyguards in less then five seconds. Damone was also skeptical of the possibility. Damone's bodyguards did not believe it, however. Bruce had even used the surprise advantage to his act. The bodyguards had seen him approaching and were ready to fight him. They quickly mounted at the door and prepared to beat him once it opened. They were wrong. The door didn't actually open as they expected. It actually didn't open at ALL. Instead, it banged on its joints and hit the first bodyguard with enough energy to knock him off the floor. Bruce was able to predict that at least one of his bodyguards would be too close. He jerked the door open. One down. Before the second bodyguard could reply, he grabbed his foot and thrust it out of his mouth. The cigarette flew past Damone, who was unsurprised. Damone turned around to Bruce who was now just an inch away, and checked his watch. Four seconds had passed.

Damone's reaction was going to resonate in Hollywood's social circles.

His popularity and fees were directly proportional. In the beginning, he raised his hourly fee to 100$. Then he increased it again to 250$. Roman Polanski was impressed with his fighting skills and his story. He flew to Switzerland with him for a private lesson.

Silliphant, Coburn, and Silliphant were his famous students back in Hollywood. They showed incredible growth and commitment. Both had made progress in it, and had also formed personal relationships with Bruce.

Bruce's students in Hollywood were able to get him small roles in various movies between 1968 and 69. He appeared on the TV series Ironside and Blondie. In the TV series "In Here Come the Brides", the actor played the role as a Chinese monk. He was also employed by various production houses as a technical advisor and sometimes as a stunts director. Green Hornet gave him the same fame as any of his other roles. Bruce felt it nearly impossible to take on the role of Green Hornet after his success with Green Hornet. There were very few roles available in Hollywood at that time for Chinese Kung Fu masters, other than a few stereotypes. Stirling Silliphant his friend and one the most important screenwriters at the time, knew that it required a unique script, written with Bruce's mind, to land him the job he wanted.

Silliphant managed, however, to get him in the movie A Walk in the Spring Rain' as the stunt dancer. Silliphant wrote Bruce a role in Marlowe. It allowed Bruce to show off his martial arts skills and athleticism. Bruce appeared only for a few seconds on screen, but this was his debut appearance in a Hollywood full-length movie.

Bruce was trying to make a name for himself in Hollywood. While he relied on the income he earned from his private tuitions, Linda gave birth to Bruce's second child. With a growing family, Bruce felt the need of a bigger home. He then began looking for a bungalow uptown in Bel Air, Hollywood. After locating it too expensive, he decided to buy a bungalow at Roscomare Avenue in downtown. It was purchased for approximately $50,000. He struggled to pay the monthly installments on the loan he used to purchase the bungalow. He was able to find some relief when he sold part of his father's Hong Kong property. Instead of purchasing furniture for his new house with the money, he bought a new red Porsche and raced along Mullhond Road with Steve McQueen.

He took great pride in the fact he had three US freestyle champions, as well as a few celebrities training under him. But he felt that he needed to make the transition to movies. Problem was, not everyone felt the same. A third problem was that producers weren't willing to take on the risk of investing in unknown Chinese Kung Fu teachers.

Bruce quickly recognized his limitations. He stopped trying to get the lead roles and instead sought a strong supporting role in a major feature film. He felt that a role as a supporting actor alongside a huge star would get him the recognition and help him open doors.

He even had an idea to make a movie in the which he was the supporting character. The movie was called 'Silent Flute'. It featured the protagonist who would embark on a journey and face obstacles along the route. Bruce, who was to play Bruce's soul voice, told him how he could get out.

He wanted Steve McQueen playing the lead role. Silliphant was asked by him to help with the movie's script. Bruce and Silliphant went to Steve McQueen's house to convince the actor to play the lead. Steve refused with a straight face that he would play the lead role of the movie. Bruce did not speak until he left. He stood out of Steve McQueen's residence and pledged to become a more famous star than him.

Steve rejected the offer and the pair went to James Coburn. James Coburn happily accepted the role of the lead. Bruce was becoming increasingly restless after Silliphant, the person responsible for writing the script, had been inactive for days. His anxiety grew to a new level after Shannon's birth, April 19, 1969. His only hope of being in a position to support his growing family was through 'Silent Flute.

Silliphant and Bruce came up with a script after many months of deliberations. James Coburn was Silliphant's assistant and he pitched the script at The Warner Brothers. The production house was happy to finance the script provided that the film was shot in India. It wanted to make use of the Indian film money it had previously made but was prohibited by the Indian government from taking out the country. Coburn, Silliphant and Bruce were both anxious about the trip.